MISFIT ₃

MISTER
JOHN

MISFIT ₃

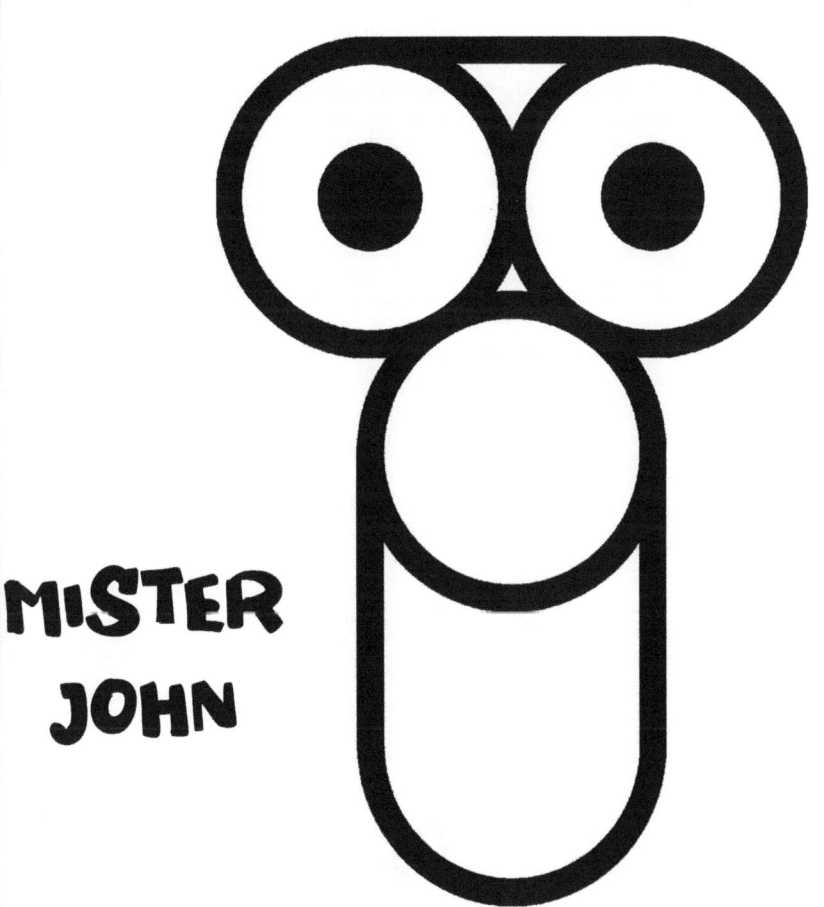

MISTER
JOHN

STORIES FROM A LIFE UNEXPECTED

First Edition
ISBN: 979-8-9900202-6-9

Cover Graphic © John Curran
Cover Design by John Curran
Author photograph © Sue L. Harrington

Author website: misterjohn.me

Fonts:
Adobe Garamond Pro by Robert Slimbach
Bobby Donut by Wahyu Eka Prasetya

YAK Publishing
Publisher website: yakpublishing.com

DEDICATION

*

TO FRIENDS
WHO ARE MORE FAMILY
THAN FAMILY

*

TO FAMILY
WHO ARE MORE FRIENDS
THAN FRIENDS

*

TO THOSE ALONG THE WAY
WHO HELPED ME BECOME
THE PERSON I AM TODAY

*

TABLE OF CONTENTS

PREFACE

MY VOICE

The first time I heard it, I was mortified, left nearly speechless for days, saying no more than required to function or be polite. Even after I "recovered" ...my voice, I've been varying degrees of self-conscious about it ever since hearing a recording of it for the first time. "Is that... what I sound like?"

Whatever I heard in my head didn't sound like what I heard on tape. I only became aware of the discrepancy after Ma and Del bought me a tape recorder, something I just had to have as a Christmas gift. Eventually, I wore out that contraption, recording anything and everything... other than my voice.

I held out hope after big people told me my voice would change with the coming "change." That change came during fifth grade, when, for a few days, I sounded like I had a severe case of laryngitis, hormones strangling me. I figured if my throat was that bad, hormones must be doing some major renovation, so my voice would be that good once I got it back. Ummm, no. I only needed to say a few lines before I knew my voice hadn't changed as hoped or even at all. I was stuck with what I had, there no second coming of puberty, no second chance for a better voice.

Knowing how my voice sounded to others and hearing it in my head every time I spoke, it was hard to ignore. Sort of the same problem dieters have when compared to people with an addiction trying to quit their habit, because while one can live without booze, drugs, or cigarettes, food… not so much. I couldn't avoid my voice. It followed me everywhere like an out-of-tune shadow. Worse, Del and Jay were everywhere, with their more than radio-worthy voices reminding me, unintentionally, that mine was not.

The only voice-related thing I had going for me was volume, as I could scream louder than most anyone. There was little call for it unless I entered an Arkansas hog-calling competition. That my voice was all quantity and no quality frustrated me because I liked the radio thing. Sitting in the studio with Del or Jay, what they did seemed like something I'd enjoy doing, but I didn't have the voice for it.

At least I realized early on that I lacked the proper skill set because I hear too many working in the media who are not as self-aware or don't have a friend with the stones to tell them to find another career. I didn't have that problem because, like my voice, my harshest critic was always right there with me - me. However, I was hardly my only critic, the child version of me seemingly not doing much to the satisfaction of others, even the things I couldn't do anything about.

I talked funny, I walked funny, and some told me I looked funny. That worked for me, though, when it came to imitating cartoon voices, as I already sounded like an animated character. Years later, those cartoon voices served a practical purpose, helping me, the teacher, get my point across when my words, spoken as me, couldn't, but could when said as Kermit the Frog, to a classroom of English as a second language speakers.

As for my walk, although it seemed a genetic thing, as others in my family walked on their toes with a bounce, I worked on my gait. More conscious of the speed and manner with which I put one foot in front of the other, I smoothened my stride. Even my looks improved, with time, enough for me to grow into my head because I only ever changed my hairstyle, which didn't make much difference.

But my voice? There was nothing I could do about that. It was what it always was: a "problem." Knowing I didn't have a voice for TV or radio, along came middle school, where I discovered I had a suitable voice for print. This learned after writing stories, mostly fiction, for Mrs. Winkler, my sixth grade English teacher, she apparently so desperate for something to grade that she handed out writing assignments seemingly every day.

Fifty years later, getting serious about writing only after I turned 50, I finally felt I'd gotten as good as I could and would get. Good enough, publishing books became a real possibility and then a reality. Tempted to become an author years before I did - the urge strong - I resisted, thanks to my speaking voice, not wanting to publish until I was sure my writing voice, the one I could do something about, wouldn't embarrass me.

Waiting wasn't easy, but I had the good fortune to encounter a book by an author who'd rushed to publish, which helped. That book was bad, and that wasn't just my opinion, as Sue struggled to finish after I put it down after only one chapter. Even so, I kept a copy to remind me not to publish until my writing voice was one readers would want to hear. After countless hours writing and editing my stories to make it so, I've listened to that voice for several years... it now your turn...

STOP ME IF YOU'VE HEARD THIS ONE

Every now and then, when it's been too long since Sue's had reason to thwack me upside the head, I ask, "Did I ever tell you about the time I was offered an upgrade from coach to first class on a KLM flight from Chicago to Amsterdam?" then shoot her a cheesy grin.

<THWACK!>

Ahhh... that's better!

Technically, Sue and I never dated in the United Arab Emirates because that would've been illegal. Instead, I had a "stalker," my description a running gag with a co-worker, Kevin, after he noticed the regularity with which Sue and I were joined at the hip, even on vacation.

"So... was your stalker on your flight to Spain?"

"It's like she had a copy of my itinerary."

"Seated next to you?"

"Yes."

"Stayed at the same hotel?"

"She did. Same room, too."

"Just the one bed?"

"How'd you know?"

"Same return flight?"

"Adjacent seats. Don't know how she does it."

Traveling with Sue, I soon discovered the joys of a traveling companion. While I never minded flying alone, there was no one to watch my luggage while I did something other than lugging my bags around an airport. And on the plane, I was always sitting next to some weirdo. Well, someone was sitting next to a weirdo.

For me, traveling across nine time zones between the UAE and Wisconsin, the journey took three flights totaling almost 20 hours, two layovers, and a car ride at each end. Across ten time zones, Sue's journey was even longer, her flights totaling more than 22 hours. Why, after Sue started "noticing me" and I started "noticing her," we thought traveling together was a good idea since we were mostly going each other's way.

Not only did we watch each other's luggage in airports, but on the plane, we shared food, drinks, footroom, and armrests - although one of us was still sitting next to a weirdo - as we sat together for hours on end enjoying each other's company. Proof we got along in such close quarters is not that we once rode a bus for 33 hours from Calgary to Minneapolis but that we did it twice.

Sue and I first coordinated our travel itineraries during the summer of 2003, flying together from Dubai to Chicago via Amsterdam. In Chicago, we split up, Sue continuing to Calgary while I took a puddle-jumper flight to Appleton, Wisconsin. Flying east to west, we chased the sun, making for a long day, but the jet lag and the trip weren't so bad traveling together, mostly.

While I always looked forward to my trips to the States, I was none too eager to fly back to the UAE, with or without Sue. Not only was my vacation over, but flying west to east meant it took two sunsets to get to the UAE, and the jet lag was that much worse. In addition, oppressive heat, humidity, and overeager taxi drivers awaited me once I stepped outside the Dubai airport terminal.

Why, every year, I bought a lottery ticket for the last draw before my departure date, hoping to win. If I did, in addition to returning to the UAE with an upgraded ticket to first class, I could collect my things and my cats, then tell my (former) director he could kiss my ass, and the millions of dollars would've been most excellent. Instead of all that, my tickets rarely matched even one of the six numbers drawn.

That first summer traveling with Sue was no different, including my buying a losing lottery ticket. After my puddle-jumper flight from Appleton to Chicago and a hike across northern Illinois, Sue and I met up in O'Hare's Terminal 5, the international terminal, for our flight to Dubai via Amsterdam. Not traveling on the same ticket, we couldn't check in together, why I approached the check-in counter with Sue standing just off my shoulder so we could clue in the ticket agent and get her to sit us together.

After handing the smiling lady from KLM my ticket and passport, she informed me the flight was overbooked, followed by words I didn't hear after hearing the word overbooked. Once I processed that dreaded word, I asked her to repeat what she'd said, hoping it would sound better the second time. And it did because what I didn't hear was not that she was going to bump me but that she was offering me an upgrade. I couldn't believe my ears.

Afraid I'd lose the upgrade if I asked for another repeat just to be sure I'd heard what I heard, I didn't ask, especially since this was not an upgrade to business class but to first class. With the flight to Amsterdam on a

Boeing 747, the upgrade was not to the front but to the top, the iconic hump that made a Boeing 747 a Boeing 747. I always wondered what it would be like to sit up there, but I never had the money necessary to find out. Now, I had an opportunity to do so on a lengthy transatlantic flight.

Not counting my first ever plane ride, in a Cessna, with my Uncle David at the controls, the only time I didn't fly coach was the time Northwest upgraded my classmates and me to business class returning from a summer study program at Oxford University in England. Yes, I went to summer school, once, at Oxford, so I didn't feel ashamed or stupid.

After an additional week of study in Paris, our group was up well before sunrise for an early morning flight to Detroit from Charles de Gaulle Airport, only to discover Northwest Airlines canceled our flight. There was no reason given, just canceled. No reason. Cancelled. Not even an apology from Northwest.

Forced to wait in the terminal for a dozen hours, Northworst "generously" provided us with the most inedible meal anyone has ever set before me, worse than even Del's infamous Tater Tot Casserole. Served in a room off the main concourse, one of the airport staff looked at me as he exited the room, shaking his head side-to-side as in, "Do not eat what I set on the table."

He knew what he wasn't talking about, the stench alone driving most of the group into the concourse even before taking a bite. A bite I took, immediately spitting whatever it was onto the floor. Following the "food" fiasco, our group probably set a record for Toblerone bars consumed in a departure lounge by the time our evening flight departed.

Northwest gave us an upgrade to business class for our trouble. It was the least they could do… so that's what they did because our upgrade was not on the nine-hour flight from Paris to Detroit but on the 45-minute flight from Detroit to Chicago. The puddle jump hardly provided enough time to enjoy the added legroom, much less any other business-class amenities. Although on a hot and humid summer day in Detroit, the complimentary cold drinks the flight attendants served us upon taking our seats were most welcome.

"Bit muggy today, isn't it?" I remarked as business people filed past on their way to coach, looking uncomfortable dressed in their suit-and-tie attire, while our group sat in the extra wide seats, wearing shorts and T-shirts, sipping on cool drinks with little umbrellas - the ice cubes that much colder in the shade. Smart-assed college kid? Yes, one determined to get the most out of his limited time as a big shot. And maybe exact some measure of revenge for all the times the suits did the same to me as I was herded through business class on the way to coach with the rest of the cattle.

Years later, still feeling like I got cheated on my only ever upgrade, the smiling lady from KLM's offer to upgrade my ticket to first class, to the hump in a 747, would more than compensate for Northwest's slight, if not that meal - nothing would make up for that meal. There was just one problem. Since Sue and I were technically not traveling together, I asked the smiling KLM lady if her offer would include Sue's ticket.

"I'm sorry, sir, no."

As much as I wanted to see what flying in style was all about in the wonder that was the hump on a 747, I thanked the smiling lady from KLM, then politely declined her generous offer so Sue and I could sit together, in coach.

When I approached the counter, I'm sure the smiling lady from KLM figured she was about to make a customer's day, one of the few times a ticket agent has such an opportunity. But I declined. No doubt she had a second, but not a third, opportunity to upgrade another customer because who in their right mind would refuse such an offer? The weirdo sitting next to Sue, in coach, that's who.

I'll probably never get another chance to fly in the hump, even if I could afford it, what with airlines retiring 747s from service, their four-engine configuration making them more costly to operate compared to modern twin-engine jets. That said, turning down my only opportunity to do so turned out to be a better story than accepting it. That's what I tell myself anyway.

Better story or not, passing on the once-in-a-lifetime upgrade to sit with Sue was one of the wiser decisions I've ever made as she and I are still sitting together, whether in coach, on a bus, or on our living room sofa. Because to this day, I believe if I'd chosen the hump, I would've been the chump, sitting by myself… then... and now.

074

I KNOW IT'S NOT CANCER

There was no reason to feel the way I did. I never felt that way before. I've never felt that way since. And I've never been a worrier. When people would ask me why I always seemed not to have a care in the world, I'd tell them I didn't need to worry... Ma did enough for the both of us. But I was worried that afternoon, with Ma and Del on their way home.

Nowadays, the entire route between Minneapolis and Waupaca can be driven on divided highways, but that was not an option back then. Two-lane highways have inherent risks, but winter weather, farm machinery, deer, darkness, and drunk drivers made them even more dangerous.

Even after Del retired and moved to Waupaca, the trips continued, albeit less frequently, because we still had family in the Eau Claire area. And there was still more family in not far beyond Minnesota who rooted for a purple football team and, in winter, often had matching purple lips.

Despite the sometimes awful winter weather, in what had become a yearly ritual, Ma and Del celebrated their day-after-Christmas wedding anniversary in Minneapolis, where they'd visit Del's oldest child,

Wayne, his wife, Sue, and their three children if they were around - Tony, Gretchen, and Rachel. Between all the chitchat, the four of them would dine at a fancy restaurant, take in a show at the Guthrie Theatre, and do some after-Christmas shopping.

The Christmas before their 16th wedding anniversary, Ma, Del, and I celebrated the holiday as usual - on Christmas Eve. We went to church to watch the always unintentionally hilarious children's Christmas program because every year, there's this one kid... and that year was no exception.

A prime rib dinner with all the fixings followed, and of course, there was an array of holiday desserts to choose from chilling in the basement and the garage. If you've never lived where freezing to death in winter is a possibility, the basement and the garage came in handy at Christmas when more cold storage space was needed.

After dinner and the dishes were done, we opened gifts. Del got Ma a pile of presents as usual, but I only remember the can opener. I know, but Ma never had an electric can opener, and she wanted one because she was finding it increasingly difficult to open cans with a hand-powered version.

So, on Christmas Day, Del installed the can opener under an overhead kitchen cabinet. It was a simple job, so simple even Del could do it. He wasn't the most mechanically inclined, but still an infinitely better option than having Ma give it a go. Del got the can opener installed all right, but somehow, he hurt his shoulder using the screwdriver. I know, but his injury didn't seem bad, so he and Ma were off to Minneapolis the next day to celebrate their anniversary.

A few days later, knowing they were on their way home from Minneapolis, I was sitting on our living room sofa, anxiously awaiting the sound of the automatic garage door signaling their arrival. I don't know why, but all afternoon, I had the uneasy feeling something was wrong, something was very wrong. The falling snow that could make the drive even more dangerous only stoked my growing fear that something was wrong, something was very wrong.

As the seconds ticked the time, the more I expected the first sound I'd hear would not be the garage door opening but the telephone ringing. So when the first sound I heard was the garage door, I breathed a sigh of relief, mocking myself for making much ado about nothing. But as soon as Ma and Del walked in the side door from the garage, the knot in my stomach returned. From their facial expressions and body language, I could tell that even though they'd arrived home safely, something was wrong, something was very wrong.

Del's injured shoulder was hurting enough that he'd skipped dinner and the theatre in Minneapolis. So, while Ma unpacked their suitcases, I would drive Del to town to see what we could find in the way of extra strength pain medication until he could get a doctor's appointment. That I would drive, Del always in the driver's seat if he was in a car, foretold the seriousness of his condition, one about to become all too clear.

Del had a presence, a commanding presence. If his magnetic personality didn't get your attention, his golden voice did. But sitting next to me in the car, that presence, his presence, was eerily absent. In the pause, after I'd backed out of the driveway but before shifting into Drive, I realized the Del I'd known since I was seven years old… was already gone.

As we pulled away from the house, staring straight ahead, Del broke the awkward silence, "I know it's not cancer." Except Del knew it was… and now I did too.

BEST TEACHER EVALUATION EVER

"I do four shows a day and matinees every other Wednesday," I told those who asked what I did at United Arab Emirates University. And that's what I did - whatever it took to get my point across. From Day 1, I recognized teaching in the UAE was not business as usual, even more so when teaching the local ladies.

For starters, in every class, some students knew little if any English, and in the early 1990s, many had never seen a computer. So, not only to get but also to hold their attention, I did whatever worked, discovering my cartoon voice impressions were particularly popular with the ladies who loved animated movies and TV shows. I also made faces, funny faces, cartoon faces, à la Jim Carrey, to help say what I couldn't in Arabic. And, as always, I talked with my hands, "animating" my voice.

When desperate measures were called for, I jumped on top of desks, screamed at the top of my lungs, and talked to passers-by in the hallway... or out the classroom window. One day, to make my point, I even ran head-first into a wall... for some reason, I don't remember what my point was. Able to bend it like Gumby, I also did silly walks, a la Monty Python's John

Cleese. I buttressed those antics by wearing colorful clothes, sport shoes, and loud ties - the fish ones popular with the students, the faculty, not so much, but then they weren't my target audience.

Animated in nearly everything I'd say or do in the classroom, there was a practical side to putting on a good show because one of the first things I learned about teaching was, "Make learning memorable, and students will remember." They were also more likely to go to class if it was fun. Since I couldn't teach students who weren't there, I strived to make my class engaging.

I thought this was especially true since my students were learning in a language far different than their own, which is not easy because the mind tends to wander when it doesn't understand what's being said. Why I did whatever I could to show, not just tell my students what they needed to know. Whenever possible, I exaggerated visual examples to help my students see the point I was attempting to make since students who couldn't understand what I was saying were essentially deaf.

I was comfortable "performing" such antics, even though others would've shuddered to do something similar in a class full of Emirati women dressed in black. Why, when supervisors who recognized my success in the classroom asked if other teachers could observe me, I hesitated, knowing what worked for me might not work for them, at best, and at worst, get them fired. I did what I did only after building a solid foundation of trust with my students.

That helped because I was never sure what would happen most nights, thanks to a network administrator whose arrogance was matched only by his incompetence. Why our computer system rarely worked as it should, if at all. At night, the network was even more unreliable because if there was a problem, the man responsible for fixing it (the same one responsible for creating it) had already gone home.

That was a problem because I taught afternoon and evening classes all my eight years at UAEU. Before each semester, when the supervisor asked for volunteers to teach evenings, I was often the only one with a hand raised out of a staff of 100 or so. Like Captain John, Mister John was happy to do the jobs no one wanted to do, knowing that it was good for job security. Volunteering also got me an off day every other Wednesday (Friday), my schedule made by an appreciative supervisor. A three-day weekend every other week? Yeah, I'll teach in the dark. Mafi mushkallah! (No problem!)

I'm proud to say that I received overwhelmingly positive evaluations from my students in my fourteen and a half years of teaching. Early on, though, too many of my colleagues attributed my success to… my looks, particularly my long hair, as one young lady gushed, "Sir, you look like Italian football player!"

While I hadn't been a teacher for long, as a student for 22 years, I had plenty of classroom experience. I knew what I liked, what I didn't, what worked, what didn't, what to do, and more importantly, what not to do. In addition, as the son of a teacher, with numerous other teachers among family and friends, I had "experience" that didn't show on my resume.

I felt better, though, when I started to get recognition for my efforts in the classroom that had nothing to do with my looks, much of that coming from my work volunteering to help new teachers adjust to teaching at UAEU. Offering tips, tricks, and even sample lessons for newbies, colleagues saw I was more than just a head of long hair. Word got around, especially after I allowed some to observe me in the classroom. I felt vindicated, which mattered to me, at least in the eyes of those I regarded as top-shelf teachers, the ones I observed in and out of the classroom.

I also liked teaching nights because the students who took evening classes generally had a more relaxed attitude, matching their teacher's. And, in a country that did not yet have satellite TV or the Internet, they were students who appreciated getting a show along with an education. So I gave them both, one geared to help them understand, even if their English wasn't so good.

A situation I appreciated more after watching Indian films on Dubai 33 TV many a Thursday (Saturday) night. I could see the action, and while I could hear it, I might as well have been deaf, not understanding a word of dialogue. Some films were subtitled, but most were not, and even for the ones that were, I was always struggling to keep up as I read.

Why I was a huge fan of Sridevi, Hindi cinema's first female megastar. Sure, she had the exotic good looks one would expect of a Bollywood actress, not that I ever noticed, but what mattered most was that I could understand her, not because I understood the Hindi, Kannada, Malayalam, Tamil, and Telugu language films she starred in, but because that woman could talk... without saying a word. With her ever-expressive face and not-so-subtle body language doing the translating, I was more or less able to follow the movie's plot, for her scenes anyway.

That I could follow along convinced me there was a method to my madness in the classroom, an opinion supported by the teacher evaluations I received from my students, matching those of my supervisors. But for all the positive reviews I received over the years, none ever topped the one given to me in class one night by a young lady named Maryam.

Always sitting in a back row corner, a favorite spot of mine as a student, we were off to a good start before she said a word. And she didn't say many, one of the quieter students in class. Probably because, like many students, she didn't want to show how much English she didn't know, or at least thought she didn't.

One of the tipoffs she knew enough was that Maryam laughed louder than anyone at my antics, indicating that she could figure out things watching me the same as I did watching Sridevi. During orientation, I cautioned new teachers, "Just because a student knows English, doesn't mean they're smart, it just means they know English… and vice versa." I suspected Maryam was one of those vice versas, clever, just didn't know much English.

Starting at seven and finishing fifty minutes later, it was the last class of the evening. With the network working like its administrator, intermittently, we were struggling, but making our way through the lesson, I doing my best to keep everyone's spirits up when we ran into glitches. I don't remember what I'd done, but having just finished my latest silliness to get a point across, Maryam, her hand over her mouth, knowing she probably shouldn't, still blurted out, "Mister John! You like cartoon!"

The class exploded in laughter, turning their attention first to Maryam, then to me, standing in the opposite corner, to gauge my reaction. What they saw was their teacher laughing louder than any of them, including Maryam. After class, though, Maryam hung back, then approached my desk, with some hesitation, fearing she'd not shown her teacher proper respect in a country where teachers were still afforded some.

"Mister John… I am sorry."

"No need to apologize, Maryam."

"No, sir?"

"No, Maryam. What you said was the best thing any student has ever said to me. Shukran (Thank you)."

With her toothy, ear-to-ear smile, Maryam left my class happy that night, as did I, and we all had a story to tell, one I still remember. That's my kind of class.

076

THAT CRAZY GUY ON THE BUS

Ma didn't own a car until she was 28. That was probably a good thing since she didn't get her driver's license until she was 28. While I got my driver's license at 16, I didn't own a car until I was 29, after I moved to the United Arab Emirates and bought a Honda Civic DX, Third World version, new, for $9000. Until then, I walked a lot, but then I was used to walking because Ma didn't own a car until she was 28.

I didn't own a car because when I was a university student, I couldn't afford one, as almost all my money went toward my education, a computer, and a camera. I still have the education And, even if the computer no longer works, and a digital camera and then another replaced the film camera, they were all solid investments as I got more out of those than I ever would've out of any car I couldn't have afforded then, long since rusted to dust in a junkyard.

Sure, there was wear and tear on my shoes, but walking was cheap, always going my way, and ready whenever I was. Moreover, as an architecture major, walking was an excellent way to see all those little building details I'd miss if I were driving or even riding the bus.

Anywhere was within walking distance if I had the time, but sometimes I didn't. Or the temperature was twenty below zero. Or the snow hip deep. Or my journey uphill, both ways. Then I hopped on the bus, and with one of the country's highest-rated bus services, the Milwaukee County Transit System, I had no trouble getting where I wanted to go, even if multiple transfers were required.

For the same reason I (mostly) enjoyed riding buses in Ecuador, I (mostly) enjoyed riding buses in Milwaukee because, along the way, I'd see a lot of life. I also saw a lot of Milwaukee, a city with a definite German flavor, owing to the many immigrants who made it their home in the mid to late 1800s after fleeing the 1848 German Revolution.

Those immigrants had a profound impact on the city. The most noticeable, besides the food, "Mmmm… bratwurst…" was how clean Milwaukee was, especially for a city its size. Cleanliness doesn't just happen. It results from a population with the proper attitude. Shortly after moving to Ecuador, we were told a former mayor of Loja, disgusted with the litter in his otherwise beautiful city, more or less told residents, in Spanish, "Just because we're poor doesn't make it OK to litter." Thanks to the mayor-inspired attitude adjustment, Lojanos cleaned up their act and their city.

One snowy afternoon, riding the 30 bus on Wisconsin Avenue, Milwaukee's main drag, an older woman with the proper attitude was seated beside me. Seated across from us was a young man needing an attitude adjustment after thoughtlessly throwing his gum wrapper to the bus floor. Banging her cane next to the bright yellow Juicy Fruit wrapper, the woman reprimanded the litterbug, "THE WORLD IS NOT YOUR TRASH BIN!"

At least, I think that's what she said, her words smothered in a thick German accent. Whether or not the young man understood her words, I do not know, but he sure got the message, picking up the gum wrapper without a word of protest. I like to think he never littered again, especially if an older woman with a cane was within reach.

No matter where I was going on the bus, if I saw something interesting, I could get off at the next stop, investigate whatever it was, and then wait a few minutes for the next bus. But if I saw something worth a longer look while riding "the dog," a Greyhound bus, I couldn't get off at the next stop because the next bus might not come along until the next day. That's a long time to sit outside a gas station, doubling as a Greyhound bus terminal, on the outskirts of Kewaskum, especially if the temperature was twenty below zero, the snow hip deep.

Running between the University of Wisconsin-Milwaukee campus on the city's northeast side and downtown, the 30 buses were always the oldest in the MCTS fleet, the newer buses reserved for the less-traveled routes. Naturally. Even so, as a major route, 30 buses ran all day and well into the night, so even if I was downtown late, I had a ride back to campus.

When I went downtown for a Milwaukee Bucks basketball game, the ride home would be late. After the game, if I joined my friends at Major Goolsby's Sports Bar or the Hyatt Hotel, my bus ride home would be even later, when muggers were out, muggers who, on Wisconsin Avenue, victimized a couple of my friends, amongst others.

While I felt safer on the bus than on the street, after midnight, there was always that one guy on the 30 bus, the crazy one no one wanted to sit next to. You know the type - always seated toward the back because crazy people don't ride up front... unless they're driving.

He had long, scraggly hair and a beard as if he'd been hired by central casting to play the part. He'd manspread, taking not only his seat but also those on either side. Not that anyone would ever sit next to him - bus passengers usually choosing the seat of least resistance.

To make the ride "entertaining," he'd carry on conversations with invisible people... "Earth is one bitchin' planet... am I right?"

He'd express nervous tics... <DRUM SOLO>

He'd sing along with songs on the radio... "Roxanne, you don't have to put on the red light. Those days are over; you don't have to sell your body to the night. ROXANNE!"

But was that crazy guy on the bus crazy? You tell me because in the six years he rode Milwaukee County Transit System buses, no one ever mugged, hassled, or threatened him. I know because for the six years I lived in Milwaukee, riding the 30 at night alone, I always made sure that crazy guy on the bus... was me.

077

DOES IT HAVE A DOCK?

I lived in Florida for eight months because I didn't want to live there for nine. Floridians like to brag about their nice weather, in January. They're noticeably quieter about it come July. FYI, a "swamp cooler" is not an exotic umbrella drink.

They pick and choose what weather to brag about. While they'll happily tell you about their sunny skies and delightful temperatures, in the winter, you'll never hear them boasting about the summer heat and humidity. Or the hurricanes. If I lived on a giant sandbar, I probably wouldn't be talking them up to prospective beachfront homebuyers, either.

Floridians like to brag about their beaches. OK, some of them are nice. Some are really nice, but they let people drive on others. As a result, the hard-packed sand on those beaches is just a few Stuckey's away from being an I-75 Alternate Route.

Pecans! 500 Yards!
Pecans! 400 Yards!
Pecans! 300 Yards!
Pecans! 200 Yards!
Pecans! 100 Yards!
Pecans! 50 Yards!'

Stuckey's - Exit Now!

Turn Around! You Just Passed Stuckey's!

And they neglect to mention the sharks waiting for unsuspectings to go for a swim. When I lived there, one young couple went for a swim and ended up splitting up... the hard way. But resign yourself to the relative safety of the beach - look both ways before crossing that compacted sand - and be prepared for an assault on your eyes. Why? While the state often promotes itself with images of bikini-clad babes, the reality is more geezers in old catcher's mitt skin oozing out of their speedos and one-pieces.

You can't un-see that. Never. Ever. And you'll see a lot of that because Florida is a popular retirement destination. I guess those retirees figure they won't live long enough to find out if scientists are right about global warming. With the average elevation of South Florida less than 50 feet, if the oceans do indeed rise, Miami high-rises might end up as nothing more than navigational hazards for ships on their way to the port of Orlando.

While the state is not so high, geographically speaking anyway, when I lived there, its crime rate was - seven of the "top" ten cities in the States for crime in Florida. I made a detour home from work one night to mail a letter, only to hear what I later found out was a guy getting knifed to death in a back alley. I didn't know exactly what was happening then because the "discussion" was in Spanish, spoken far more rapidly than I could translate at 3 am after working a 12-hour shift.

Despite living in the Middle East and South America for many years - and you know how dangerous those places are - that's the only time I was ever a stone's throw from a violent death that wasn't a government-sponsored execution. And I got up at 4 am to get a front-row seat for that. I didn't just happen upon it.

And speaking of Spanish, "¿Hablas Español?" While you can "Press 1 for English" on the telephone, there is no way to do that when you're out and about in Florida. And you might want to because Sue and I agreed we heard more English in Cancun than in Miami despite Cancun being located in a Spanish-speaking country.

Floridians sometimes "adopt" that Spanish to make things sound better than they are, for example, palmetto bugs. I discovered a nest of them outside the cracker box house where I lived during my second semester at the University of Florida. Rocks with legs, the palmetto bugs were huge, most at least two inches long, scurrying about the sidewalk after I exposed the nest in an adjacent rock retaining wall.

I tried stepping on them. That didn't work. I tried riding my bike over them. That didn't work. I finally got a hammer, smashing one on the sidewalk. That stopped it, long enough for it to look up at me as if to say, "That all you got?"

"Palmetto bugs?" Yes, palmetto bugs, because I'm sure it sounds way better to tourists than "giant fucking cockroaches." They're Florida woods cockroaches, and when threatened, they can eject a most foul-smelling spray up to three feet. Well, there it is…. It also explains why they're sometimes called skunk roaches, stink roaches, or other smelly names.

Then there are Florida's Alligator Crossing signs. Take them seriously, very seriously. Chances are you won't encounter one, but if you do… At least you'll know exactly what you're dealing with because some of the state's other dangerous creatures are not so easily identified. Here's a tip: Generally speaking, many of those hard-to-spot predators have one thing in common - they carry a handful of business cards. While that's enough warning for most people, there are always a few, P.T. Barnum building a career on them.

"I have swampland in Florida I'd like to sell you."

"Does it have a dock?" And I'd ask that question because I find swamps interesting.

If you ever changed schools when you were a kid, who wanted to be your friend on your first day? More than likely, the kid nobody else in the school wanted for a friend, and with good reason. But even as an outcast, they knew what you didn't and tried to take advantage of that and you for their benefit.

Nobody needs to get "schooled" like that - here, there, or anywhere. So my apologies to the good people of Florida for picking on their state to make my point, because anywhere you've ever or never been has its good points and bad, along with a few people looking to take advantage of you - people who will tell you the truth, the whole truth, and nothing but the truth... you want to hear.

078

DINNER AT NOORA'S

What had been a pleasant conversation turned testy. Even though they spoke in Arabic, I could tell Oumi, her grandson Eisa, and his younger sisters Alia and Noora were getting caught up after not seeing each other since… the previous Friday. While I didn't know what Oumi was upset about, I knew with whom she was upset, Eisa. To emphasize her displeasure, she began rapping her cane on the floor, keeping the beat for the rhythm of her diatribe.

Noora must've sensed my wonder, as she then explained, "Oumi's upset because my brother still isn't married and isn't any closer than he was last week!" Filed under "Everything's Funny Until it Happens to You," I chuckled, knowing why Oumi was unhappy, as she felt the young man was too old to be a bachelor. Noora's explanation and my reaction took the heat off Eisa because Oumi then turned her attention to me after Noora told her what she'd told me, adding that I, too, was not married.

Directed at me, I didn't need Noora to translate Oumi's question, "How old are you?" answering, "41," Noora then translating for Oumi. As I was almost old enough to be Eisa's father, Oumi again began rapping her cane on the floor, giving me the same "what for" in Arabic she'd just given Eisa, not approving of my bachelor status either.

I could've told her about Sue, but in the United Arab Emirates, I didn't want to draw attention to the laws the two of us were breaking - we still a decade and another country away from getting married. Instead, I smiled, nodding in agreement to the beat of the Oumi's rapping, the rest of her family getting a good laugh, she the beloved character she was.

That character expressed itself in Oumi's face, as she looked every bit her age and then some, born years before oil was discovered in the UAE when life was hard. From what I heard and saw, Oumi helped keep the family grounded, her presence reminding them to appreciate all they had because she could remember when the family had next to nothing.

One of those things the family had was a stretch Mercedes limousine, green, and the number on the registration plate was just two digits - 14. The family's quirky Pakistani driver had been driving Oumi (Miss Daisy) around Dubai for 25 years, wherever and for as long as he pleased in that elongated car.

Sitting in the back, if Oumi thought she'd been out and about too long, she'd rap on the glass divider with her cane, "I want to go home!" He often ignored her, getting Oumi out of the house perhaps more important to him than even Oumi or her family. Nevertheless, when Oumi went out, she was always prepared, carrying a white shayla, medicine, chocolates, and perfume in her bag.

I had the good fortune to meet Oumi thanks to Noora, a former student of mine, one who stood out from the get-go, she... different... highlighted by her competing in a Dubai mini-marathon, the first local woman to do so in a country where women weren't encouraged to compete in athletic events, especially in public.

In my classroom, I found it hard to find fault with Noora, not just academically. She was an absolute delight to have around - courteous, helpful, friendly, and not just toward me but other students. Bright, in more ways than one, if I'd had any children, I would've felt fortunate if they turned out anything like Noora.

With everyone acknowledging her excellence at almost everything, she was a three-time candidate for a Student of the Year award - an award Eisa won at Dubai Men's College and Alia at Dubai Women's. Noora wanted nothing more than to match her older siblings. Somehow, during her three years as a Higher Diploma business student at Dubai Women's College, she never won, even though no student did more and more for the college when I taught there.

When I had a vote, Noora won on her first opportunity - she the obvious choice. However, some faculty believed a more "typical" student should win, so she lost after management mysteriously extended voting. The winner was a good student, a good person, and also one of my favorites, but her resume didn't come close to matching Noora's.

Two years later, Noora's last chance came and went with yet another loss. The student who won was excellent academically but nothing more, there no extracurriculars on her resume. When she was my student, she was a pain in the ass, the only student I ever contacted my supervisor about, as she pouted for days after 9/11 because I didn't put an end to her classmates' desire to discuss the event, one she found embarrassing to her culture, her religion, and, apparently, herself. After my supervisor, Tony, pointed out that such discussions were exactly what an institution of higher learning was for, she grudgingly agreed to retract her protruding lower lip.

She was still a pain in the ass. And that wasn't just my opinion because before she graduated, an older sister of one of her classmates, who studied medicine in Europe, told me she'd heard what a pain she was. "From what my sister says, it sounds like that uptight bitch needs to get laid!" If you think those women in black were quiet, shy, lacking in opinion… some were.

After hearing that Noora had lost and to whom she had lost, I made inquiries, trying to get to the bottom of another injustice that didn't concern me… but did. I even went to Noora's supervisor, asking why she lost, especially to someone who had contributed nothing to the college beyond the minimum. "Politics," Monica sighed, she no happier over the situation than I.

Disappointed Noora didn't win, and why, I was also surprised, given who her father was, a longtime friend of His Highness Sheikh Nahyan bin Mubarak al Nahyan, Minister of Higher Education, and Chancellor of my current employer, the Higher Colleges of Technology, and my previous employer, UAE University. Shaikh Nahyan was, at the time, one of the few UAE cabinet ministers not a son of His Highness the President Sheikh Zayed bin Sultan al Nahyan.

Noora's father had wasta (who-you-know clout), and plenty of it, not that his children needed it to win awards, they more than capable on their own. Nevertheless, this wasta, I believe, hurt Noora, as there was a perception among too many that she already had everything. Yes, she did, but that was no reason to deny her what she'd earned, all on her own.

I have no use for entitled people, but Noora was not one of those, as demonstrated by her not making a fuss over losing to lessers, as she could've done, as another student with her inherited wasta might've done. Instead, Noora accepted her defeats gracefully, although I know it bothered her that she never got the recognition she deserved, feeling betrayed by the college to which she had contributed so much.

After I started teaching at Dubai Women's College, Ma visited every year for a month or more. I was pleased she had the opportunity to spend time with Noora, especially when she was around for the college's annual bazaar, when, for a week, classes were suspended as students operated on-campus businesses of their making. The resulting atmosphere was a mini version of Dubai's annual Shopping Festival.

When Noora invited Ma and me for dinner at her home, there was no hesitation in saying, "Yes." I'd never been invited into the home of an Emirati before, certainly not for dinner, nor with a former student. Ma was thrilled over the unexpected opportunity, as was I, but not without some trepidation, I wondering what might be for dinner because, you know, "I'm not eating that!" and all.

Much to my relief, dinner that night featured chicken with stuffed peppers (no mushrooms), made not by a maid but by Noora's mother, Naima. I'd never had stuffed peppers, but it is now one of my favorite dishes. There were also plenty of sides, typical of any Arab feast, such as stuffed zucchini and spring rolls, along with Chinese and Egyptian rice, my favorite. As was also typical of any Arab feast, dinner was merely the appetizer, we then moving from the dining room to the majlis (sitting room) for an evening of conversation filled with coffee, tea, and desserts.

Ma doesn't drink coffee anymore, but she did then, sampling the Arabic version, flavored with cardamon.

She expected Turkish coffee, which she said was bitter and strong, so she preferred the Arabic, as it seemed lighter, with less caffeine. Never having had a cup of coffee, it was tea for me.

For dessert, there was mahalabia, a gelatin made with milk and sugar infused with rosewater, popular during the holy month of Ramadan. There was, of course, baklava. Always baklava, but there was also barazek, a Syrian-Palestinian cookie, more a thin cracker, the main ingredient sesame, coated with honey, ground pistachios, and sesame seeds.

Our conversations were possible because every member of Noora's family present spoke English, except for Oumi. I quickly learned Oumi, like my favorite Bollywood movie starlet, Sridevi, didn't need to speak English for me to understand her. As for the rest, I was always fascinated with Arabic speakers who spoke English as well, if not better than I, the languages so different... and I managing, but still struggling, with the far more familiar Spanish.

Later in the evening, after losing track of Ma, I found her in a corner of the majlis with Noora's uncle, Ebrahim, a sweet soul if ever there was one. I knew their conversation was a serious one - they sharing photos, both with tears in their eyes. During the drive home, Ma told me the two of them had struck an unexpected friendship, commiserating over family lost to cancer - Ma, an older and younger sister, along with a husband, and Ebrahim, a cherished daughter.

It was an evening of getting to know one another without the typical Western distractions of alcohol, TV, smartphones, politics, or religion. At evening's end, after spending hours in a house with people so different in almost every way that can be labeled, I couldn't help but think how much more we had in common. For starters, good food, good conversation, and grandma were all important… and all-important.

When Noora's older sister, Alia, married, she invited Ma to her reception. While Ma got a second chance to visit Noora at her home, that night I settled for visiting with her and Naima outside their villa, they stepping outside to greet me since I couldn't enter the ladies-only affair inside the family villa. They did this when I dropped off Ma and again when I arrived to collect her for the ride back to Sharjah.

Ma spoke mostly with Naima, while I spoke mostly with Noora. I don't remember much about what was said, but I do remember, all made up, wearing her sister-of-the-bride dress, how stunning Noora looked because she did indeed have it all, including good looks. I knew out there, somewhere, was a young Emirati man wandering around, oblivious to how fortunate he would be. He knows now, as last I heard, Noora was married, with children, adult children by now.

When I went to pick up Ma, Naima offered to have their driver take us back to Sharjah in the family limo, the stretch Mercedes. I politely declined only because I would've had to taxi my way across Dubai to recover my Jeep. I should've accepted anyway and would've, just for the story, if I'd known then that, years later, I'd be writing books… of stories.

079

SOMETIMES, YOU JUST KNOW

"I'm about to send you a lot of money. I've never met you. I've never even been to South America, much less Ecuador. How do I know I can trust you?"

Our lawyer in Ecuador laughed. But there was something in the way Grace laughed that told me I had nothing to worry about when most everyone would've told me otherwise. Sometimes, you just know, even when there's no reason to do so other than a reassuring laugh. All I know is that I slept better that night than I had since we first heard of the property off a dead-end dirt road near Vilcabamba.

While we were in Haida Gwaii to check out the islands and do some crabbing - it was a vacation after all - we were also working the deal for the property in Ecuador. It wasn't easy doing that in Masset, mainly because, in 2006, the Internet was new to Haida Gwaii. While Scott and Jo had a boat, their getaway place had no Internet service.

There was only one Internet café in Masset, which wasn't even in Masset but in the First Nation's village of Old Masset, a mile or so up the road. Sue and I would venture out to Old Masset late in the morning, hoping to catch the café open for the lunch "crowd." Quite often, it was still closed when we arrived. We'd ask around if anyone knew when or if the café would open. What we got, mostly, were puzzled shrugs.

After our trip to Ecuador, Sue and I concurred that the residents of Haida Gwaii would do well there because they have much the same attitude toward life as their southern brothers of separate mothers. Both cultures work to live. Neither live to work. And in Haida Gwaii, they work just enough to live and not one minute more. As a result, many island businesses open only when the proprietors feel like working.

One of our favorites was a small café on North Beach a ways past The Elephant Pen, the Moon Over Naikoon Bakery. It was open in the mornings until the woman who ran it ran out of food. So if you showed up at 10 am only to find the cinnamon rolls were all gone... It sucks to be you. Come back tomorrow... a bit earlier. She made her money and then spent the rest of the day doing whatever she wanted. We filed her situation under "Role Models."

Having Internet service provided in a remote part of Canada on a whenever basis was one more obstacle we had to overcome. We didn't need more stress, trying to close a real estate deal for a property in Ecuador involving an owner we'd never met, now residing in Uruguay, and our lawyers in Ecuador, that we'd never met. And, transferred from a bank in the Channel Islands to a bank in Wisconsin was our money, to send south if we decided to buy the property.

Waiting on the porch fronting the Internet café, we enjoyed the view of the Masset Inlet. The ravens skulking about were huge... and spooky... in an Edgar Allan Poe sort of way. They had a look about them that said, "You're not from around here, are you?" And then there was the totem pole carver across the road.

Watching him sculpt a considerable cedar log helped pass the time until the café doors opened, if they opened.

Despite the waiting around, and some days waiting around for nothing, the cafe not opening, we got done what we needed to. Our trip to Ecuador was all set. Our lawyers had all the required paperwork ready to go. Our money was in place, so if we decided to buy the property, there'd be no delay. We just needed to get there to check it out.

While our time on Haida Gwaii ended on schedule, it was much too soon. We were sad to leave but knew we'd be back. We packed Art's pickup truck with our bags, a chest freezer filled with a small fortune in crab, salmon, and halibut, and a generator, chugging away to keep the freezer's contents frozen.

This time, it was just a 90-minute drive to catch the ferry, not a 20-hour odyssey after our flights from Dubai. The return trip on the ferry to Rupert was again smooth, but back on the mainland, the weather turned nasty. Driving in the dark on the winding two-lane highway alongside the Skeena River was tricky enough without the pouring rain that started shortly after we left Rupert.

Driving in B.C., even in the summer, can be an experience. We ran into some flash rainstorms in the mountains. While the three of us shared the driving on the way out, on the way back, except for one short shift driven by Sue, Art drove the entire way. He insisted, perhaps because of the seafood treasure loaded in his freezer.

But as long as the generator kept chugging away, we were in no hurry to get to Calgary. Good thing because the weather insisted we take our time. And we did, taking an even longer route back to Calgary so Sue could meet up with an old friend in Kamloops. Yes, Kamloops. It's a real place. A nice place. Really.

Art was a happy man after we made it back to Calgary with his still-frozen seafood. While he ate his share, I'm sure, he had more fish and crab than he could ever eat, his surplus "currency" he used for trading in his good ole boy network, most of the deals negotiated in the alley behind his house. We, too, were happy because our first-ever visit to Haida Gwaii was one we'd never forget, having already provided us with enough material to fill our summer holiday scrapbook... and our journey had only just begun.

080

YES!

"Imagine what it must sound like outside of town."

Not sleeping on the bed firmer than the floor at Vilcabamba's Hosteria Jardin Escondido, we heard the roosters cock-a-doodle-doing… all night. Middle of the night rooster banter featured prominently in Ecuador's soundtrack, even in town as we were. So, it seemed fitting that we had eggs for breakfast.

Just as we finished our toast at the hosteria's restaurant, the man Lee arranged to show his property arrived and introduced himself. Lee would have preferred to meet us, but he'd already moved to Uruguay, and his first alternate had just moved to Montañita, a town on Ecuador's coast. We hoped it wasn't an omen that the only gringos we knew of living in Vilcabamba no longer did.

So Lee's second alternate drove us out to see the property. He told us that the warm and breezy weather was typical for the dry season. The river valley was still 50 shades of green. We wondered how lush it must look in the rainy season. As we headed down the winding one, one-and-a-half, sometimes two-lane dirt road, the sheer beauty of the surrounding scenery transformed us into mouth-breathers.

To our left was Mandango Mountain, "The Sleeping Inca," a former vacation location for Incan royalty. We knew from Lee's photos that his property had a great view of Mandango from the backyard, one we were now even more eager to see. As the anticipation mounted, we passed the Monasterio Puerta del Cielo (Heaven's Gate Monastery). We chuckled over the name (after I translated for Sue) because we figured we'd entered heaven about a mile back. After turning in and out of a ravine just past the monastery, there it was, Lee's property.

With walls painted adobe orange and the window trim a deep blue, the clay tile-topped house peeked over a weathered red brick wall. We parked in front of the blue steel gate framed by an arch of bougainvillea. Lee would later tell us he had the prickly plants cut back before he left for Uruguay, not thinking how it would look to prospective buyers - dead. We didn't care.

Passing through the gate and under the bougainvillea, we set foot on an acre-and-a-half of dream-come-true. Barely onto the property, Sue and I already knew what we'd suspected since we saw Lee's brochure - that his property was our property. Of course, we still had to do our due diligence, so we puttered about the upper property, making sure all was as advertised. And it was, and then some.

Lee was concerned his brochure had oversold his property, pumping it up too much. He hoped we weren't traveling from Dubai for nothing. His concern was understandable, given that a woman had come from the States to check out the property just the week before but decided not to buy. She thought it too rustic and, for a woman living alone, too remote.

The photos in Lee's brochure showed a house that never had a full-time resident in its 40-year history.

Two of the bedrooms, constructed of rammed earth, were original, the walls a foot and a half thick. The third bedroom, the bathroom, and the covered but open-air kitchen, all added later, were made of brick. There was also a large covered patio area and a car park. Near the drop-off to the lower property was a small guesthouse, a converted chicken coop.

Lee had not oversold his property. If anything, he'd undersold it, as we were about to discover. Making our way down the 111 steps to the lower property, we began to see what Lee had left out of his brochure - almost everything in the nearly 200 yards between the upper property and the river, starting with the bamboo grove at the bottom of the drop-off.

Even though we were only halfway down the 60-foot slope, the bamboo soared above us in all its majesty. Some six inches in diameter, the culms knocked together in the breeze, creating the largest set of wind chimes I'd ever seen or heard. We just stood there... gobsmacked... at the bamboo... and that Lee had not included a photo of such a stunning feature.

Oversold? Not after we passed a second bamboo grove and a wide assortment of fruit growing on the property, including banana, plantain, oranges, sour oranges, mandarin oranges, limes, lemons, sweet lemons, guayaba, avocado, maracuyá, mangoes, grapefruit, berries…. and coffee. Coffee! Spindly plants with little green beans were everywhere. Excited? Yes! And I'd never drunk a cup of coffee in my life.

After so many years living in the desert, I wanted water, a property with lots and lots of water. The first time I met Lee in person, he told me he never received so many questions about water until I sent him my first email inquiry. His property had irrigation canals, a hand-dug well near the river, and the Vilcabamba River, forming the southern boundary. Municipal water would arrive at the gate within two years.

By the time we reached the river, Sue and I had seen more than enough, so when our lawyers arrived from Cuenca - Grace and the other half of the legal team, her husband, Nelson - their timing was perfect. From the smile on Grace's face as she saw Sue and I sloshing about in the clear and chilly Vilcabamba River, I think she already knew the answer before she shouted from shore, "Are you still interested in buying the property?"

"YES!" Sue and I replied in perfect harmony without first consulting each other. It was that kind of property. As demonstrated the week before, it was not a property for everyone, but it was for us. That doesn't mean you should buy a property five minutes after seeing it on your first day in a country or continent without seeing the nearest town in the daytime. Only crazy people do that. But if you do your homework as Sue and I'd done, five minutes was all it took for us to open the door when opportunity knocked.

After we returned from Ecuador, I called my Aunt Rita. She and my Uncle 'You guys gotta buy this!' David were most curious to know what had transpired in Ecuador. So, of course, I played it coy, talking about everything but Ecuador until she could stand it no more, blurting out, "So, the property in Ecuador. Was it everything it was advertised to be?"

"No, it was not…" I replied, rather glumly, "…IT WAS WAY BETTER!"

Rita screamed so loud that hours later, my telephone ear was still ringing.

081

APRIL FOOL

My life living overseas began not with a trip to the United Arab Emirates but to Scandinavia. No, not any of those Nordic countries, but the village of Scandinavia, located just north of Waupaca. Barely a wide spot in the road, I'd only ever passed through on my way to the only slightly wider village of Iola to attend their annual old car show. While Scandinavia was just ten miles distant, the drive from Waupaca was the beginning of a journey I never could've imagined.

Particularly after having tried and failed for months to find a job. Never before had I experienced such utter frustration. I had only myself to blame, as all through graduate school at the University of Wisconsin-Milwaukee, I'd focused on getting my dream job in architecture, designing stadiums at HOK Sport in Kansas City. The only job I ever really wanted, I put all my eggs in one basket, even though I knew it was a gamble. And then I didn't get the job, my heart broken, and all of my eggs… scrambled.

To make matters worse, I had the misfortune of graduating when the industry was looking to fire, not hire. When I figured my situation couldn't get any worse, it did after my college buddy, Craig, called from

Los Angeles with news about our favorite professor at UWM, Kent Keegan. He'd beaten cancer twice before, his second victory over the disease coming while I was working on my Master of Architecture thesis project. As my thesis committee chairman, I was delighted, in more ways than one, that he'd beaten it again.

A few months after I graduated, his cancer returned, again, but for reasons unknown, Kent didn't tell anyone. Perhaps he knew he didn't have it in him to beat cancer a third time. And he didn't, Craig telling me Kent lost his years-long battle with cancer on an operating table in a California hospital.

When Kent died, I lost a friend, a fan, a mentor, a favorite teacher, and, in the context of my job search, my best reference. But as bleak as my situation seemed, I only had to remember what Kent's two young sons had lost… and what Kent had lost. Nothing breaks up a pity party quite like perspective.

Even so, it was a difficult time. But during that soul-stomping winter, something my Uncle Dennis said lifted my spirits, even though when he said what he said, we were in a church basement following the funeral of his Uncle, my Great Uncle Ed. "I admire you for putting all your eggs in one basket." Knowing the high hurdles Dennis had to overcome in his post-graduation job search, his words carried even more weight, enough to carry me through that winter.

And come March, with the return of Pat and Mimi, the owners of Clear Water Harbor, I was back to work at my old job, piloting the Chief Waupaca sternwheeler. While The Harbor wouldn't open to the public for two months, there was always much to be done in preparation for the upcoming tourist season. More importantly for me, two weeks of work would result in two weeks of pay.

I was down to four dollars when Pat handed me my first paycheck that season. Four, and I still owed the bank more than $50,000 in student loans. Had Pat and Mimi remained at their winter home in Key Largo, Florida, one week longer, I wouldn't have been able to make my student loan payment that month.

I was never so happy to be back at my old job, even if I was still looking for a new one. And that spring, I once again had the good fortune of working with John, a Lieutenant Colonel in the Air Force. I always enjoyed working with him as not only did he know what he was doing, but John was friendly, funny, and always had stories to tell. I'll never forget his remark about his time serving in Vietnam, "It was so fucking humid there, from the day I arrived until the day I left, my skivvies were never dry."

But that spring, John had even more stories to tell. As an aircraft maintenance specialist, he was one of the first called to duty after Iraqi troops invaded Kuwait the previous August. So as we readied the boats, buildings, and grounds, we talked, mostly about John's recent stint in the Gulf. One country he mentioned often was largely ignored by CNN during their coverage of *The Gulf War: Operation Desert Storm* - the United Arab Emirates.

In particular, John waxed lyrical about what he saw while on R&R in a city called Dubai. "Everyone drives around in big fancy cars. The buildings are made of marble. They have so much money that they can't spend it all. It's unbelievable. You should see it!"

Until the last Friday of that month, I never imagined I would. As I did every morning before heading off to The Harbor, I scanned the classifieds in the *Milwaukee Sentinel* newspaper. If someone had told me to do this before declaring my major, I probably would've chosen something other than architecture because there were so many listings for accountants, nurses, and welders.

"Sigh…"

About to once again crumple the classifieds in frustration, the smallest of ads caught my eye.

WANTED: MAPS and COMPUTER TEACHERS

"Maps?   (As I suspected, it should have read MATH) Computers? I could do that."

  UNITED ARAB EMIRATES UNIVERSITY

"The United Arab Emirates? I know where that is!"

CALL TOM NYKL 715-555-6789

"Tom! Hey! I know him! It won't even be a long-distance call!"

Even though Clear Water Harbor was only five minutes away, I couldn't get to work fast enough.

"John! Tell me more about the UAE!"

"Why?"

"I think I have a job there!"

"No way!"

"Really! I saw an ad in the *Sentinel* this morning!"

So, after I told him about the ad and explained my connection to Tom, John told me everything he could about the UAE. Before the Internet, before Google search, John was my best source of information about the country so small that on CNN's maps, even its three-letter abbreviation was too big to fit inside its borders.

When I got home that afternoon, I called the number in the ad.

"Hello…"

"Hi, Tom!   This is John Curran, calling from Waupaca."

"John! You want a job teaching in the UAE?"

"YES!"

"OK, how about you come up on Monday for lunch? Stop at Hardee's on the way. Pick me up a big roast beef with fries and a Coke."

No Monday ever took so long to arrive, but after stopping at Hardee's in Waupaca, I was on my way to Scandinavia when it finally did. Tom had given me good directions, and good thing he did because his cabin was nestled in the woods off a country lane. It was a home one would stumble across only if hopelessly lost or looking to dump a body.

Scandinavia was already off the beaten path, never mind a cabin in the woods outside the village. The architect in me appreciated the 150-year-old cabin Tom and his wife, Sue, had recently renovated. Seamlessly adding an addition, half their home was shiny new, but stepping into the logged living room, I felt like I'd traveled back in time, about 150 years.

After I opened the bag from Hardee's, we got down to business at the kitchen table. Tom sat across from me, wearing jeans and a T-shirt. As he scarfed down a big roast beef, I did the same, trying desperately not to spill ketchup on my best suit. My only suit. I never felt so overdressed as we sat there, eating drive-through fast food at a kitchen table in a log cabin.

Other than my suit, the interview was informal, but Tom and I had known each other since I was a high school student. The first time I met Tom, he was a colleague of Ma's, a math teacher, my math teacher at Waupaca High School. He worked his students hard. Why, once a month or so, some student suffering from equation overload would say, "Mr. Nykl, we don't feel like studying math today," as the rest of the class rushed to support their courageous classmate.

"Yeah. Let's do something else today, Mr. Nykl."

Tom almost always said, "OK."

When he did, he'd go off on another subject, usually physics-related. We'd all end up learning something, just not math, or at least not the math in our textbook or the curriculum, because Tom was always teaching, even when we asked him, and he agreed not to.

Our math class never got to say goodbye to Mr. Nykl because one day, a former student, just released from juvenile lockup, made his way to the high school… looking for trouble. What he found was Tom attacking him for no other reason than he was a teacher. The thing was, this loser and Tom had never met. Before the day was over, Tom turned in his resignation.

Although disappointed, I couldn't blame him, especially since I knew Tom had better things to do. Because for a year and a bit, I felt fortunate to have someone I regarded as a university professor teaching my high school math courses.

While I was always good at math, I never liked it much outside of geometry class. I liked it even less when math became more of a lesson in Greek, but Tom had a way of keeping me interested, even liking math. So much for that.

It would be five years and three universities after Tom resigned before I would see him again. Sitting in a physics class at UW-Milwaukee, I heard a familiar voice in the hallway.

"…Tom? …Tom!"

I could hardly wait for the class to finish. When it did, I bolted for the door, but by then, the voice was gone, so I roamed the halls, poking my head into every office. After several pokes, I found him sitting at his desk.

"Tom Nykl! What are you doing here?"

"John Curran! What are you doing here?"

We exchanged stories to answer our matching inquiries before we both had to get to class. While I ran into Tom a few more times that semester, once my physics class was over, it would be another couple of years before our paths would again cross on my way out of another building after an art history class.

"John Curran!"

"Tom Nykl! This isn't the physics building. What are you doing here?"

Tom had a new office in a new building because he was heading a new program to raise the skill set of disadvantaged incoming students so they could attend and compete at the university level. Even though our conversation was brief, I could tell Tom was happy in his new line of work.

It would be a couple-two-three more years before I saw him again, at his cabin near Scandinavia, where he interviewed me for a job in his latest endeavor - raising the skill set of incoming students at United Arab Emirates University. Seems some Emirati Shaikh got wind of Tom's program at UWM and wanted him to implement it at UAEU.

Like Tom, I probably could've shown up for our interview wearing jeans and a T-shirt because, like our previous encounters on the UWM campus, it was more a friendly get-reacquainted session than anything. I had the feeling that I only needed to show up on time, get his Hardee's order correct, and a job would be mine. And it was, as I returned home that afternoon with a contract in hand.

Overjoyed, it didn't matter to me that *The Gulf War: Operation Desert Storm* had just ended. It didn't matter to me that the UAE was conveniently located between Saudi Arabia and Iran. It didn't matter to me (pre-Internet) I knew almost nothing about where I was going. My job search was finally over.

Not only was it over, but I'd also gotten the job I wanted, even if I'd only been aware of it for four days. I had no hesitation in agreeing to accept the position because I saw teaching at UAE University as the opportunity of a lifetime, something no technical college in Thief River Falls, architect's office in Grand Forks, or even the one in Kansas City, could ever match.

After arriving home, I told Ma the most excellent party-on news before calling family and friends.

"Hey! I got a job!"

"Congratulations! Where?"

"The United Arab Emirates!"

"The what?"

"The United Arab Emirates. The UAE. I was hired to teach computers and math at their national university in the desert oasis city of Al Ain!"

"No way!"

"Really!"

"No way!"

"I'm not making this up! How could I?"

"John Curran, I don't believe you!"

This conversation was repeated more than once that evening. No one could, no one would believe it. The reaction of my family and friends was almost as frustrating as not finding work for so many months. Almost. So after I was done making calls, I decided if I were ever again hired to teach in the United Arab Emirates, I wouldn't tell anyone about it… on April Fools' Day.

082

RANIA

My "stupid human trick" - writing my name on the whiteboard in Arabic, then in English backward, and then in English backward and upside down - helped me make the first impression I wanted on the first day of a new school term. More than that, the resulting reactions I "drew" from my new students helped me assess the prospects for the coming weeks. Little did I know what the future held for one young lady who caught my eye.

The first time I saw Rania's big brown eyes and smiling face, she was seventeen going on eighteen, sitting four rows back on the left side of my classroom. Wearing a dress I later learned she sewed herself, Rania provided a colorful contrast in a room otherwise full of Emirati ladies covered in their black shaylas and abayas. Rania was not wearing the local dress because she was not a local but a Palestinian.

Not all students at United Arab Emirates University were Emirati, as there was a small but noticeable contingent of international students from countries as far west as Morocco and as far east as Indonesia, making for a diverse, thus more interesting campus. While all the students were Muslim, the clash of cultures was sometimes problematic, especially when it came to wardrobe choice. Some more conservative students were more than a little judgmental when it came to those not dressing liberally enough.

The day I saw Rania for the first time was the first day of my second year teaching on the Women's Campus at UAEU. She stood out in the classroom in more ways than her dress and dresses. Over the years, I had a few, a very few, smarter students, but none with the same steely determination I'd seen in my restaurant-owning friend, Dan.

Not only to succeed but also to help others, becoming my unofficial teaching assistant roaming the room as I did. With 25 students but only two feet, two ears, one mouth, and one brain, Rania's help was most appreciated. My rules were that she couldn't do the work for them, nor could she assist in Arabic - they had to learn their lessons in English as was required.

Rania's English was good, she one of those students with whom I could carry on a conversation that wasn't haltingly awkward. One day during office hours, as we were discussing language, in English, of course, Rania surprised me by relaying her frustration with my first language despite her proficiency. "Mister John, I am very good with Arabic. I even write poetry. But in English, I find it difficult to express myself. It is frustrating."

Here in Ecuador, every time I speak to someone in Spanish, and my Spanish will never be as good as Rania's English, I'm reminded that whatever eloquence I have speaking or writing in English, I lack in Spanish. Try as I might, I'd never be able to express myself as fully or accurately in another language as I do in my own. Even though I never imagined it could be a problem for Rania, given the relative ease with which she spoke to me in my mother tongue, her explanation made perfect sense.   Hers was a lesson I've never forgotten.

They say never make fun of someone speaking broken English because it means they know at least one other language you probably don't. Also remember that even if they know English well, like Rania, they might still find it difficult and frustrating. The subtleties of language are many - why people can come across as rude or even stupid when expressing themselves in a second or third language. I know I must sound like an idiot when speaking Spanish, humbling when the waist-high Ecuadorian neighbor kid does not… I'm guessing.

Despite whatever issues Rania had with English, she scored 100% in my computer class. While some students versed in the material would coast, often resulting in silly mistakes because they figured they had it covered, Rania was meticulous; there'd be no mistakes on her watch.   "She'd make a good accountant," I thought to myself.

Why I smiled a year or so later when she told me she'd changed her major from business to accounting. Even so, Rania still completed her degree at UAEU in just three and a half years. She told me how the other students teased her because her auntie must work in administration, putting her on the fast track to a degree. Rania didn't need any auntie because she had me, more than willing to help a student eager to help herself.

Late that first quarter, we both learned that in the second quarter I'd be teaching third and fourth-quarter courses for students who'd failed them the previous year. Rania asked if she could attend. Even though I told her there was no guarantee I'd be able to make her grades count, she tripled up on her computer course load with the hope of finishing the first-year university program in just two quarters, she already well ahead of schedule in Arabic, English, and math.

After the mid-year final exams, I met with the program director. I explained the situation, figuring my best chance to get Rania's unorthodox matriculating to count would be to ask at the last minute. With a coming surplus of students and the resulting shortage of teachers and space, that we could "rid" our program of a student seemed a marketable plan.

I could've counted all of Rania's teeth when I told her the director agreed to permit me to add her marks to my grade sheets - 100% in all three courses - ensuring she'd finish her first year in only half a year. And she did, graciously thanking "auntie" for his help.

Part of Rania's motivation to finish early was so she could graduate and get a job to help her family. In the early '90s, many Emirati women had little opportunity, need, or desire to get a job. That was not the case with Rania and many other international students like her, so I gave them extra attention. Why I continued to help Rania whenever I could, even though she was no longer my student and accounting was definitely not my specialty.

Like when she stopped by my office looking for help with statistics, she knowing I'd completed some courses in the subject on my way to earning a B.A. in economics along with my B.S. and Master of Architecture degrees. In particular, she wanted help with a miserable DOS (ask an older person) statistics program called *STAT 101*, which I taught whenever management scheduled me with math courses.

Despite the software and hardware (an IBM PS/2 Model 30 286 desktop computer), Rania and I shared a delightful afternoon working through statistics problems. One of the few times this Mac guy since

1988 ever enjoyed working on a PC, and *STAT 101*, the person sitting beside me was the only reason why.

Rania was the kind of student teachers dream about. If all my students had been like her, I would've gone home far fewer nights with headaches and sore throats. The only concern I ever had with Rania was her weight. Slight in stature when she was my student, a year or so after she no longer was, I noticed there was noticeably less of her. Why I encouraged her to eat more - Rania's heavy workload eating away at her.

I never remarked to another female student about their weight in thirteen-plus years teaching women in the UAE, but that was the kind of relationship Rania and I had. She knew her health was suffering, and I could relate - my workload as a university student contributed to my hair turning gray. Hair that returned to brown within months of my graduating for the third and final time... and has remained brown ever since. <SUE EYE ROLL>

Despite our closeness, as Rania's graduation day approached, I wondered if it would mark the end of our teacher/student relationship-turned friendship. I didn't think we'd see each other anymore, but more than that, I didn't know if we'd have much to talk about after we no longer had UAEU in common. Little did I know that the friendship I thought might be nearing an end was just getting started.

083

YOU'RE PICKING UP THE CHECK

Living on the wrong side of the tracks for so many years helped keep me grounded. That and only months before, I had over $50,000 in student loans to repay and but four dollars to my name. Why I was forced to borrow $20 from Ma just to take the lovely Elizabeth on a date. Big shot? Not. Even though workers were astounded at the (relatively) enormous size of my villa, especially since I had no wife or children. I couldn't believe it either - my new home at least two times larger than any place I'd ever lived. The master bath was larger than my dorm room at UW-Milwaukee, which, by Wisconsin state law, could be smaller than a prison cell.

University faculty were among Al Ain's highest salaried foreign residents in the desert oasis city on the edge of the Empty Quarter, and the Westerners, about half of our department, were easily the most visible. Why, as a white American male hired to teach at the national United Arab Emirates University, some regarded me as a privileged character.

Nevertheless, I didn't take my recent status upgrade seriously, even though I almost always walked around with a thousand or so dollars worth of dirhams in my wallet. I wasn't trying to be a big shot, but the UAE was a cash society back then. An oh-so-safe one, my colleagues and I walking around with "Monopoly money" without care that we'd be robbed. However, some of my coworkers at UAE University had a more difficult time adjusting to their newly acquired status and relative wealth, perhaps the snobbish behavior of some of our Emirati students rubbing off on them.

All one had to do was examine the vehicles in the parking lot outside the Men's Campus at UAE University to know there were those with more money than an education. While most faculty members drove bottom-of-the-line Honda Civics, many Emirati students drove Mercs, BMWs, or fully outfitted SUVs - the modern-day camels, but then many students had more status than faculty.

Some had so much more that they didn't even drive, even though they owned a vehicle, probably several. A fact I became acutely aware of after learning one of my students was a son of His Highness Shaikh Zayed bin Sultan al Nahyan, Ruler of Abu Dhabi, President of the United Arab Emirates, and, at one time, the world's wealthiest man.

I drove myself to the university in a Third World version of a Honda Civic while his chauffeur drove him to the university in a stretch limousine, a Mercedes. Another sign of status was a single-digit license plate, or no license plate, as was the case with his limo. At least I got to drive... yeah, let's go with that.

While vehicles were an obvious status symbol, less visible was the help one could afford to hire. It was common for privileged characters to hire servants of all kinds, including maids, nannies, drivers, gardeners, cooks, cleaners, and laborers... even "girlfriends." Sad to say, those "with" too often treated those "without" like... the help.

A few times, students treated me like the help as there'd be that one Emirati who'd snap their fingers when they wanted my attention. While I didn't appreciate a student treating me the same way they likely treated their help, I viewed any such occurrence as something a good teacher is always on the lookout for - a teachable moment.

Mine began with an admonishment, "Don't you snap your fingers at me," in my sternest teacher voice, the same one I use to tell our neighbor's dogs in Ecuador to "Shut up!" at three in the morning. On the Women's Campus, that teachable moment continued with me pointing toward the omnipresent cleaning ladies, the help, from "shithole" countries, dressed in their sky blue overalls, then giving my class a lesson not in the syllabus.

"See those cleaning ladies? They're here all day, from seven in the morning until ten at night. But being here is better than what they have when they go home at night, crammed into dorms not nearly as nice as yours.

Even though most of you don't get out, you get to go home on weekends and maybe go out with your family. The university doesn't allow these cleaning ladies to go anywhere except once every two weeks when their supervisors take them downtown. They get to shop for two hours, but most don't need the time because they can't afford much with what little money they're paid.

And many of these cleaning ladies are better educated than you. They just had the misfortune of being born in a country with few opportunities. So they left their home, family, and friends behind for a chance to earn a living... cleaning up... after you. So don't you snap your fingers at me, and especially don't you snap your fingers at them. Treat everyone as you want to be treated."

Word must've gotten around because I only had to give that lesson a-couple-two-three times.

Like the cleaning ladies on the Women's Campus, the help hired by the two Western hotels, the Hilton and the InterCon, endured considerable hardship. They also worked long hours for a pittance and lived in housing that made my college dorms seem like, well, the Hilton or the InterCon.

They surely didn't need privileged characters like me making their lives more difficult. But one night, a colleague of mine did just that. We sat around an outdoor table on the patio at the InterCon's Horse and Jockey pub, enjoying the first pleasantly cool evening of the school year. As the two hotels were the only Western oases in Al Ain, the few Westerners in the city frequented each frequently.

As our evening neared an end and we wanted to get the check, a co-worker snapped his fingers at our waitress... and proceeded to make matters worse by speaking to the young lady as if she had no more feeling than a stone. After she walked away, our table turned on the finger snapper.

The Yank (that would be me) squawked, "What the fuck was that?"

The Canuck politely posed, "Who are you to be snapping your fingers at anyone?

The Brit authoritatively stated, "You are a maths teacher from Michigan, not the bloody Queen."

The Aussie just said, "Dude!"

Then we all pointedly told him, "Tonight, you're picking up the check."

084

THE TOOLBOX

I'd hoped to get the deed done, unnoticed, after Ma went to bed. What I hadn't counted on was the sickly smell exhaling from the oven being so overpowering it would fill her bedroom, in the opposite corner of the house, why she was up and in the kitchen and in my face to investigate.

"WHAT DID YOU PUT IN MY OVEN!"

"A toolbox."

"A TOOLBOX!"

"It's for a school project."

TIP: If your mother is yelling at you for what you're doing, even if you have children, tell her it's for a school project.

This time, though, what I was doing really was for a school project, in shop class. For my freshman year at Waupaca High, there were 12 weeks of drafting, 12 of woodworking, and 12 of metalworking. I thought the last would be what I'd like least. Instead, metalworking turned out to be my favorite.

Maybe because I made something I still have, something useful. That something was a toolbox, constructed of sheet metal, the pieces cut, bent, and then spot-welded together by me in the Industrial Arts building. All the sturdy steel box needed was a coat of paint. Green, I decided, and then spray-painted.

So what was the toolbox doing in Ma's oven, creating such a stink? Baking, of course. Well, the paint, anyway, to give it a hard enamel finish. I preheated the oven as high as it would go, 450F, then placed the toolbox on the rack inside and closed the door. Within minutes, the smell of baking oil paint was way worse than that of drying oil paint. Who knew?

After graduating high school in 1981, the toolbox went wherever I went to university, the box just the right size to hold my modest tool collection. It was still modest ten years later when I was packing my belongings to move to the United Arab Emirates. I debated whether to include my toolbox and its contents as it was heavy. Paying by the pound to air freight 17 boxes from Appleton to Abu Dhabi, weight was money.

The toolbox made the move anyway, one of the better decisions I've ever made because two weeks after arriving in Al Ain, I had tools, my tools. While the contents of those 17 boxes helped me feel like I was not as close to the end of the world as I was, the box containing my toolbox was the first I opened.

I'd been in my newly constructed villa for a week, but despite the new villa paint smell, there were odd jobs that needed doing, jobs requiring tools. And I didn't much care for what I'd seen my first two weeks in the UAE - the selection was limited, and the quality suspect. Not a do-it-yourself kind of country, there was not one Lowe's, Home Depot, or Rona (Canada), nor anything similar, not even an Ace Hardware. Yet.

I made do, with a little help from my "friends" in the green toolbox. But I didn't always have the right friends as there were jobs for which I was not prepared, like working with concrete, the primary material used to build my villa. One thing I find frustrating is not having the right tools for a job. So one of the first things added to my toolbox was a four-piece concrete drill bit set (one I still have) with four matching sizes of plastic inserts for screws - the bits and inserts metric, the measurement system most of the rest of the world uses. Even though it was "Made in Puerto Rico," the packaging text was in French, and the quality was good.

Good, unlike many of the tools I bought in the UAE those first few months, "Made in China" crap I had to buy because there was nothing else. Why the second most exciting thing that happened to me during my first year in the UAE was when an Ace Hardware store opened in Dubai, off Airport Road. After it did, no trip 90 miles north was complete without a visit to Ace. For efficiency's sake, UAE University could've deposited my paychecks there.

With my near-weekly shopping stops, my tool collection soon outgrew my old green toolbox. I needed a new one, a larger one, and then bought two because they were on sale, and I knew my shopping at Ace would continue until I moved to another country or ran out of money.

Despite outgrowing my toolbox and buying two new ones, I kept the toolbox I built, as there was nothing wrong with it other than its too-small size. It was, however, just the right size to store in the trunk of my car for tool emergencies I never had with my ever-dependable Honda.

The only time I ever used my tools on that car was to put a stop to the annoying "BEEP! BEEP! BEEP!" it made whenever my speed exceeded 120kph (75mph) on the highway or a side street in downtown Al Ain. All it took was a couple of screwdrivers to take the dashboard apart and needle-nose pliers to bend the tiny metal clip on the speedometer mechanism that made an electrical connection when it rotated past 120kph.

For the next few weeks, I was the most popular "repairman" in Al Ain, "fixing" the many Honda Civics of colleagues and friends who were also annoyed by the "BEEP! BEEP! BEEP!" In addition to maybe voiding any warranty, removing the warning mechanism probably violated UAE law, but then I didn't figure I'd ever be taking a police officer for a ride. Certainly not one that would exceed the 100kph (62mph) speed limit... because that would be against the law.

When I returned to the UAE for my second stint, my toolbox was waiting for me, along with more than 17 boxes of belongings, at a friend's villa in Al Ain. Lamia, a lovely Syrian woman and former colleague at UAEU, graciously agreed to store my stuff in the extra house at her house (servants quarters for servants she didn't have) until my return a year-and-a-half later, six months later than I, and Lamia, expected.

But my toolbox wasn't packed away with the rest of my stuff. It was in the trunk of the Honda, parked in the back of Lamia's driveway. A few weeks after I returned, after I sold the Honda to a former student, Mariam - the car a present for her father, a retired fire chief in Fujairah - the toolbox moved to its new home in my new Jeep Wrangler, forest green.

A few months after that, after Sue and I started noticing each other, one of the first things I noticed about her was when she said, "I'm hungry," feed her, immediately, or she turned cranky. One of the first things she noticed about me, besides I could "grandma bake," was that my apartment doubled as a hardware store...for select customers.

Compared to other hardware stores catering to the public, mine was just two floors away, often better stocked, and always open as long as I was home. Not to be outdone by Ace, my hardware store came with its own "helpful hardware man," one making house calls… for select customers.

The toolbox moved to Ecuador, too. Sue was happy the helpful hardware man went with given the first night after we moved there, the bathroom sink started leaking, the stove broke, and in the afternoon, a cracked valve created a fountain in our backyard that rivaled the waterworks fronting the Bellagio in Vegas.

As we didn't have a vehicle that first year, the toolbox didn't have a home until the second year after we purchased a 1975 Toyota FJ40 LandCruiser. Like the Honda, the FJ, despite its age, never needed any emergency repairs, so the toolbox was just along for the ride until we bought a second vehicle, a 1979 Toyota FJ40 LandCruiser. The second FJ was not as reliable as the first, at first, although the repairs required were beyond my ability and my tools to fix.

Like the time an engine mount broke as Sue was driving up our bumpy (we aspired to smooth) dead-end dirt road. Somehow, she was able to drive it - the engine and drive train miraculously undamaged - to her mechanic's garage less than a mile away, where Wilmer had the right tools - an engine hoist, for one - to fix the problem. The FJ has rarely needed anything other than servicing since, so once again, the toolbox, like me, just along for the ride in Sue's little red wagon.

I would've painted the toolbox red if I'd known way back when. Maybe I should paint it red now. After so many years, it could use a fresh coat. Then I could bake the toolbox in our oven when Sue wouldn't be home for hours, or days, because I don't think she'd buy that "It's for a school project" excuse.

085

VEGAS, BABY!

There was a cemetery off the highway that has since been rerouted around the small town of Winchester, Wisconsin. Branching off the highway alongside the cemetery was a road, a dead-end road. Between the road and the cemetery was a sign, a yellow diamond with black lettering that read, DEAD END. I chuckled every time I drove by and saw the sign fronting the marble orchard. Someone had a sense of humor in Winchester.

On the dead-end road to Calico Basin, Nevada, there was a sign, a yellow diamond with black lettering that read, NO OUTLET. I guess that's the new terminology, DEAD END perhaps seen as too severe. But NO OUTLET was not exactly true. We could always turn around and go back. But on our way to a wedding ceremony, our wedding ceremony, the point was made. And NO OUTLET seemed a better warning than DEAD END.

After Sue and I decided to get married during an already-planned trip to Las Vegas, we knew an outdoor ceremony was what we wanted. On my way down to our lower property in Ecuador, machete in hand, I told Sue, "It's the States. It's Vegas. There has to be some entrepreneur out there who will marry us the way we want." By the time I returned, Sue, who can find anything online, had found the Las Vegas Wedding Wagon. She'd read the reviews, and all were positive, but more importantly, they seemed to do the kind of ceremony we were looking for - casual. So the who had been decided.

Next was the where. The LVWW would marry anyone anywhere in the Las Vegas area, provided it was legal, of course. While a Vegas wedding was convenient given the limited time we had in the States to get it done, we didn't want a Vegas wedding, so it was one of the LVWW's premium locations that caught our eye - the Red Rock National Conservation Area.

We'd stayed at the Red Rock Casino, Resort & Spa on the city's west side a few times before, but only because we were guests, I speaking there at conferences. We're not much for swanky hotels, not wanting to feel as though we have to get dressed up, or dressed, just to go down the hallway for a bucket of ice. While the Red Rock is a higher-end property, it seemed to cater more to locals, so it had a more relaxed feel.

While the Red Rock was everything you could ask for in a swanky hotel, it also had a bowling alley, multiscreen Cineplex, numerous restaurants, and a food court inside the casino. We always felt right at home there. More than the facilities and amenities, the people impressed us most, as the staff at the Red Rock were always helpful, friendly, and courteous, from management to the maids. Later, we discovered that Red Rock's parent company was one of the top 100 places to work in the States, the only hotel company to make the list.

The Red Rock is oriented more or less north/south, so east-side rooms have a view of the Vegas Strip, while west-side rooms have a view of the Red Rock National Conservation Area. So there was a good view and a better view, the Red Rock side the better, sometimes stunning, especially early in the morning when the rising sun hit the rock formations. Even though it was just a few miles from the hotel, we never made our way out to see it close up, but then, with no transportation, we had no practical way to get there. But thanks to the Internet and Google Earth, we had a chance to preview the area. We didn't take long to decide that the Red Rock area would be our location.

Next came the when which was the most problematic. Checking the LVWW's online calendar, they were on vacation the first few days of our stay. OK, no problem, as we would use that time to get our ceremony ducks in a row, including obtaining a marriage license. But their schedule was pretty much booked once they returned from vacation. The only open date was their first day back, and then only in the afternoon, the afternoon the conference was to start, the afternoon I was to present for an audience of over 900. We emailed the LVWW, telling them our story and our predicament.

While attempting to get the when sorted, we went ring shopping. I've never worn jewelry of any kind, even a watch, so I was less than enthusiastic about getting a ring. Nevertheless, since Sue was not a woman who needed a big flashy rock (she's a keeper), I was happy enough to go ring shopping, knowing we wanted rings reflecting how we wanted our ceremony to be and how our lives are - simple.

Fortunately, Vilcabamba was a touristy town for such a small outpost on the way to nowhere in particular in Peru, so some artisans were always hanging around hawking their wares, a few with brick-and-mortar shops.   One such man was Cristobal, from Chile, I quite impressed with his shop. Not only did I like his jewelry, I was particularly intrigued by his display cases, much of his jewelry resting on beds of beans, rice, and other assorted grains - colorful, tasteful, and matching the style of his jewelry, unpretentious. Sue and I picked out two silver bands with a simple hammer-style texture - nothing flashier than that for us. Cristobal had our rings ready in just a few days.

They say you're supposed to spend three months' salary on rings. They say? Who came up with that formula?   I bet it wasn't a financial advisor.   Or an accountant. I'm betting it was a jeweler. Three months? Really? Go to Antwerp, Belgium. DeBeers has bins of diamonds, oodles of them, but they only release so many per year to keep the price up. With a virtual monopoly on the diamond market, they can get away with that… if the public is foolish enough to fork out piles of cash for highly compressed carbon.

Shortly after securing our rings, we heard back from the Las Vegas Wedding Wagon. They were so impressed by our story that they graciously agreed to shorten their vacation by a few hours and squeeze us in before the conference began. So with the when settled, all Sue and I needed to do was get to Vegas.

086

TRAFFIC'S GONNA BE A BITCH

"What's happening?" I asked, pointing to the TV featuring a grim-faced Richard Nixon.

"He's resigning, effective noon tomorrow."

"Oh…". Not quite 12 years old, what did I care?

But I remember. And if you're old enough, you probably remember where you were on August 8, 1974, when President Richard Nixon announced his intent to resign in front of a national TV audience. I know where I was, in St. Charles, Missouri, a suburb of St. Louis. I'd just entered my stepsister Debbie's apartment after a few hours of splashing around in her complex's swimming pool. St. Louis. August. Cool pool water!

But I also remember where I was three days before, on August 5. I was at Busch Stadium with Ma and Del, watching a game between the St. Louis Cardinals and the Philadelphia Phillies. St. Louis is a great baseball town. Why, if you get the chance, take in a Cardinals game with the Gateway Arch as a backdrop on some hot, humid summer day. It's an experience, even if you're not a fan of the Cardinals or baseball.

And it was especially special that night because Cardinals outfielder Lou Brock was well on his way to breaking Maury Wills' single-season stolen base record of 104. Not only that, Bob Gibson was on the mound for the Redbirds. You could feel the energy in the stadium when Brock came to bat. And with all eyes on number 20, he didn't disappoint, banging out four hits in six at-bats and, more importantly, stealing two bases.

His first steal came in the bottom of the 6th. With Brock on first and second base open, the stadium trembled. So did the Phillies pitcher, clearly having trouble focusing on the batter, distracted by Brock measuring his lead at first. Everyone knew what was coming, so when Brock broke for second base with the pitch, the crowd of 33,476 erupted. Somehow, the roar got even louder after the second base umpire signaled, "SAFE!" Brock had stolen his 73rd base of the season.

Unfortunately for the Cardinals, the Phillies pitcher had far less trouble with the rest of the lineup. So despite allowing only four hits and one run, Gibson and his Cardinals teammates were still trailing 1-0 after the Phillies batted in the top of the 8th inning. In the bottom of the 8th, Brock got another hit, then stole his second base of the night, number 74. But when a popup ended the inning, stranding Brock on second with the Cardinals still trailing by a run, Del decided the game was over.

"We'd better head back to the motel. Traffic's gonna be a bitch."

So we exited Busch Stadium, me trudging behind, "But the game isn't over yet…"

Once inside our car in the parking garage next to the stadium, Del turned on the radio so we could hear Jack Buck's call of the game on KMOX radio. The 50,000-watt clear-channel station was one of Del's stops in his long radio and television career, a stop that came when Jack and some guy named Harry Caray were the voices of Cardinals baseball.

When the Phillies scored a run in the top of the 9th, extending their lead to 2-0, Del felt vindicated in his decision to get a head start on traffic. I was still unconvinced, in the back seat, mumbling to myself, "The game isn't over yet..."

Sure enough, in the bottom of the 9th, Cardinals catcher Ted Simmons hit a two-run homer to tie the game. Some of the excitement was lost hearing it on the radio, zipping along on the freeway, in the back seat, mumbling to myself, "I told you so..."

Neither team scored in the 10th or 11th innings. By the 12th, we'd arrived at our motel. With no local station televising the game and no radio in our room, we continued listening in the car in the motel parking lot. There were no food vendors, but at least a bathroom was close.

Brock got his fourth base hit in the 12th but was caught stealing. The next inning, however, the Cardinals won the game on an RBI single by Joe Torre. Thirteen innings played. We saw eight. Five runs scored. We saw one.

But this was not the first time Del prematurely decided a game was over. On Saturday, December 23, 1972, we watched the NFL playoff game between the Oakland Raiders and the Pittsburgh Steelers from Three Rivers Stadium in Pittsburgh. Televised by NBC, Curt Gowdy was the play-by-play announcer that day.

It was a hard-fought game as the defenses dominated. But after backup Raider quarterback Kenny "The Snake" Stabler, who'd replaced starter Daryle "The Mad Bomber" Lamonica, scored a touchdown on a 30-yard scramble with one minute and seventeen seconds left, giving Oakland a 7-6 lead, Del decided the game was over.

"We need to get going."

Fortunately, we watched the game at his parent's home on Eau Claire's north side because no one ever got out of there in a hurry. Huddled around the door to the foyer, the grownups always said their goodbyes… and then discussed everything they inexplicably hadn't in the preceding hours.

"Are we leaving or not?"

Sometimes, I enjoyed being a ten-year-old, just blurting out whatever was on my mind. While the adult yammering continued, I positioned myself to see the TV at the far end of the living room. The situation seemed hopeless for Pittsburgh. Needing a field goal to win, the Steelers were out of timeouts, there were just 22 seconds on the clock, and it was fourth down and ten yards to go from their 40-yard line. Standing in their way was a Raiders defense that had allowed only two field goals.

Down to perhaps their final play, Steelers quarterback Terry Bradshaw dropped back to pass. Under a heavy rush, he threw a pass intended for running back John "Frenchy" Fuqua. Fuqua, Raiders defensive back Jack Tatum, and the football arrived simultaneously at the Raiders' 35-yard line, ricocheting backward off Tatum (Raider fans would disagree).

"Del! Del! Look!" I said, tugging on his jacket as Steelers running back Franco Harris, following the play, scooped up the deflected football just inches above the turf. Had it not been for the extended goodbyes at the front door (aka the Midwest goodbye), I would've missed perhaps the most miraculous ending ever to an NFL game.

Del would've too, although by the time he realized what was happening, Harris had already rumbled into the end zone, giving the Steelers a 12-7 lead and, following the extra point, a 13-7 win. Dubbed by a

Steelers fan as the "Immaculate Reception," NFL Films regards the play as the greatest (and most controversial) in league history.

But it wasn't the only time Del would give up on a game where the deciding play was given a name. On Saturday, September 24, 1977, we watched an early season college football matchup between the fourth-ranked Ohio State Buckeyes and the third-ranked Oklahoma Sooners. The early season non-conference contest was worthy of a New Year's Day bowl game, the kind not usually seen in September, back then anyway.

A then-record crowd of 88,119 fans filled Ohio Stadium in Columbus that afternoon. Del and I watched the ABC broadcast at our house on Lawson Drive, just east of Waupaca. Pitting two top teams, we were anxious to see the game, but when Oklahoma jumped out to a 20-0 lead early in the 2nd quarter, Del was as restless as Buckeye fans.

"This game is over."

With that proclamation, Ma and Del decided there was no need to wait until the game was over to make their planned trip to Fleet Farm. Now, if you're not familiar with the shopping experience that is Fleet Farm, that's unfortunate, but all you need to know is this - if Fleet Farm doesn't have it, you don't need it.

"You want to go with us?" Del asked.

"No, that's OK. I'll stay here and watch the rest of the game."

History told me I should do just that. History was right because Ohio State's comeback had begun before Ma and Del would've reached the live end of our dead-end road. Over the next two hours, Ohio State turned a 20-0 deficit into a 28-26 lead. Nevertheless, it was a precarious lead as Oklahoma lined up for a potential game-winning field goal with six seconds on the clock.

"BLOCK THAT KICK! BLOCK THAT KICK! BLOCK THAT KICK!" screamed Buckeye fans after Ohio State head coach Woody Hayes called timeout in an attempt to ice Oklahoma's kicker, Uwe von Schamann. Born in West Germany, von Schamann was one of those soccer-style kickers still new to American football fans.

But just when I thought the game couldn't get any better, during the timeout, it got better. With Ohio State fans screaming their Buckeyes out, the Sooners kicker, in the middle of the field, started waving his arms... leading Buckeye fans in their cheers of "BLOCK THAT KICK!"

I'd never seen anything like it. "That German dude's got ice water in his veins." I wondered what Sooner's head coach Barry Switzer was thinking with von Schamann leading the cheers of the opposing team's fans before his game-deciding kick. Probably the same thing I was thinking, "He better make this."

With my chair pulled directly in front of the TV to be closer to the action, I watched von Schamann boot that 41-yard field goal as straight and true as any kicker could do, silencing the Ohio State crowd. After the kick split the uprights, Oklahoma running back Billy Sims said Ohio Stadium got so quiet, "You could hear a rat pissing on cotton."

Despite blowing a 20-0 lead, Oklahoma won 29-28 on what is known in Sooners football lore as "The Kick." But Del wasn't the only one who gave up on the game that day. Sensing a blowout after Oklahoma jumped to the big early lead, ABC switched its national TV coverage to regional telecasts. Fortunately, it was our regional game, so I didn't miss a thing, including Keith Jackson's call, and for college football, there was none better than Mr. Jackson.

When Ma and Del returned from Fleet Farm, no doubt with something they needed, I was grinning from ear to ear when they walked through the door and the first words out of Del's mouth were, "So how badly did the Sooners beat'em?"

"Let me tell you! There were just six seconds left on the clock…"

087

IT IS DONE

"Mister John! What are you doing? Get out of there! Now!"

"Yes, ma'am!"

While I couldn't see her face, as she was covered in black from head to toe, I knew it was Ayesha, having learned to recognize my students even when I couldn't see them. And I didn't have to see Ayesha's face to know she was giving me a look of utter disgust as she scolded me. It was rare that I let a student, even a former one, talk to me like that, but then I'd never been in this situation before.

I was in line, sort of, in a hallway at a clinic attached to Al Ain's Al Jimi Hospital, the same scary "Josef Mengele Approved" institution where I was taken for a physical during my first fourteen hours in the UAE. Running the length of the building, there was not one square foot of hallway floor visible because it was covered with sandal-wearing feet, along with one guy in Reebok Walkers.

We were so tightly packed that there was no room for both of my feet to lie flat on the floor. Parts of each were, but parts were on top of other people's feet, and parts of other people's feet were on top of mine. I'd never experienced such population density as we were standing on top of one another.

While there was a roof over the hallway, we were outside, and it was May, so even in the shade, it was brutally hot, a problem compounded by the mass of humanity. Stuck in the middle of the three-step wide hallway, the only air any of us received was what flowed through the screen of decorative concrete blocks that formed the outer wall.

Al Jimi Hospital was no better than I remembered it five years prior. I and scores of primarily South Asian workers shared a new low in patient service that day as we waited to collect our government-mandated blood test results. Despite our numbers, only one window was open, and even that one, like the other four that were closed, was covered so no one outside could see inside. Perhaps more to the point, no one inside would have to look outside at the masses packed into the hallway like canned sardines.

When a patient's test results were ready, a muffled voice yelled their name and shoved the paperwork through a small slot above a window, the papers floating to rest on the people pile. Many hands over heads then passed it along to the recipient, more than relieved to leave the hallway behind.

It was crowded, it was hot, it was uncomfortable, but most of all, it was dehumanizing. I'd never experienced anything like it, but I'm guessing most of the South Asian workers squeezed beside me had, more than a few times. Like any other day, that day, they accepted their plight, with a few no doubt wondering why I was in line with them, as Ayesha did.

After she called me out, I wished my fellow sardines well with their wait for test results and then extricated myself from the hallway. Stuck in the middle, I didn't think I could make it to either end. Fortunately, just a few "feet" away, some broken blocks in the screen provided an opening just large enough for me to crawl through.

After getting another earful from Ayesha about waiting in the hallway, I didn't dare complain about her being a half-an-hour late because she was a half-an-hour early… for an Emirati. With her scolding complete, we exchanged the usual pleasantries before she walked into the employee entrance without knocking. Two minutes later, she walked out with my completed paperwork.

"Who is this woman? How do you know her?" asked a man most forlorn, still standing on the sardine side of the screen. For the first time since I was in grade school, I slyly replied, "That is for me to know and for you to find out." While I felt a bit guilty for saying that, it was none of his business, and it was better for all concerned that I didn't answer truthfully.

From there, Ayesha and I made our way to yet another clinic where my test results would be analyzed. There was no waiting this time as Ayesha, once again, with me in tow, walked right into the employee entrance. And she could because Ayesha worked there. As far as I know, she was the first female student of mine to be gainfully employed.

The first thing she did was introduce me to the clinic's director because… why waste time with underlings? In his plush, air-conditioned office, the three of us sat in comfy leather chairs chatting, drinking tea, and eating cookies while my paperwork was reviewed, stamped, sealed, embossed, watermarked, and whatever-elsed. It was a much more civilized experience than I had at Al Jimi.

When all was said, drank, eaten, and done, I had passed a second AIDS test and had the paperwork to prove it. It was the third clinic I'd visited to complete the required AIDS test to get my UAE residence visa renewed. Yes, third, because before the hallway at Al Jimi where the blood was tested, and before the tea party at the third where the results were analyzed, there was the clinic where the blood was taken. One test. Three clinics.

I was not happy I had to go at all, especially when the rules had only recently changed, requiring the test for visa renewal. Of course, the rules changed. It was my turn. After seeing Al Jimi Hospital on my first day in the UAE, I went to great lengths to never set foot in a hospital or clinic of any kind in Al Ain, so discovering I had no choice did not sit well with me. Unlike the first time around, when I had help with the tests and paperwork to get my residence visa, this time, I was on my own.

At the bloodletting clinic, the line was long but moving along. The nurse was an older Sudani woman. It appeared that her job was to do nothing more than sit in her chair behind a small white table all day, drawing blood from patients. Since the line appeared to be an all-day line, you might think that with all that practice, she'd be good at her job. I did... and I was wrong.

I'm about as white as white can be without being dead. I'm not a doctor or a nurse, but I'm pretty sure I could locate my veins - those greenish-blue lines all over my arm. But this nurse could not find one. Not on the first poke, the second, the third, the fourth, or the fifth... After the sixth, she started poking the needle around under my skin, hoping to hit something, anything. After a dozen or so back-and-forths, she still hadn't hit a vein.

Perhaps thinking I was the walking dead, she pulled the needle out before she stuck me again, repeating her back and forth inside my arm at least another dozen times before she finally hit a vein. I was never so happy to see my blood. After she was finished, the cotton ball she handed me didn't seem nearly enough reward for all the needling I received.

As I was leaving the clinic, eager to put as much distance as I could between myself and the bloodletter, a South Asian worker strode alongside.

"You American?"

"Yes."

While his attempt to befriend me was glass-transparent, I cut him some slack, knowing I would soon be out the door and on my way. Realizing his time to schmooze was short, he got straight to the point with his newly found "friend."

"Please tell me… how I get green card?"

I stopped, turned, and replied, "I have no idea. You need to ask someone who is not an American citizen."

Hearing my answer, then realizing the flaw in his befriending me, he sheepishly replied, "Thank you, sir."

The following day, my arm was black and blue from my shoulder to my wrist. At work, a colleague and I compared notes. And arms, Henry's, from shoulder to wrist, black and blue too.

"Sudani nurse?"

"Yes."

But after three clinic visits and a passed AIDS test, all that remained was to submit my completed paperwork, my passport, and 500 dirhams ($136) to my employer. UAE University administration would then deal with immigration to get my soon-to-be expired residence visa replaced with a new one. The wait was usually a month or more. While I wasn't planning on going anywhere anytime soon, I never liked to hand my passport to anyone, especially for a month, living where I was.

Fortunately, I didn't have to because Ayesha told me she and her friend, Alia, would take care of it for me. At first, I resisted as I had doubts about allowing former students to handle my visa renewal, a process involving my precious passport. If something went wrong, the only person I would have to blame was myself, but Ayesha and Alia insisted to the point that I knew they'd be offended if I refused what was a generous offer.

They instructed me to bring my paperwork and passport to the campus the next day, where I handed them my paperwork and passport… and 500 dirhams.

"You keep your money, Mister John."

Thinking they would pay the fee for me, I insisted on giving them the money.

"You keep it, sir."

"Are you sure?"

"Yes, Mister John." Ayesha didn't have the most patience, and I could see she was getting that "Why are you making this more difficult than it needs to be?" look about her.

"But I don't want you ladies to pay."

"Do not worry, Mister John. No money is needed."

"OK, ladies, if you are sure."

As Alia put my paperwork and passport into her designer purse, I happily returned the 500 dirham bill to my wallet.

"How long will it take?"

"Bukra inshallah (Next week, Allah willing), Mister John."

"Of course! Shukran (Thank you), ladies!"

"Mafi mushkallah (No problem), Mister John."

Two days later, Ayesha and Alia stopped by my office, unexpectedly, with smiles far too big for my liking. When I saw their faces, my heart stopped because they had that all too familiar look young Emirati ladies got when they knew they were about to get an earful from an angry teacher.

However, when Ayesha pulled my passport from her purse, my heart restarted, "It is done, Mister John."

"Really?" I opened my passport to make sure it was. It was. I found the old visa, canceled, and then the new visa. While I was pleased to have my visa renewed and my passport in hand, especially after only two days, I had some questions.

"Are you sure you don't want me to pay you 500 dirhams?"

"No, sir. We did not pay. See? No postage stamp."

Sure enough, in the upper left corner of the visa, where a 500 dirham postage stamp was supposed to be affixed to show the visa had been paid for, there was only a bit of Arabic script stamped in black and a signature.

"Ladies, this will be OK?"

"Do not worry, Mister John."

"So when I pass through immigration, they won't make a problem for me?"

"No, sir. Promise."

"Whose signature is this where the postage stamp should be?"

"Do not worry, sir, no one will question it."

And for the four years I used it, no one ever did. However, every time I passed through immigration at the Dubai airport, I got puzzled looks that said, "Where did you get this visa?" No officer ever inquired, though, not out loud anyway. They were as impressed with my residence visa as some of my Arab colleagues were at UAE University.

"How much did your visa cost?"

"Nothing."

"Nothing? I spent 3000 dirhams ($816) getting my family's visas renewed! How long did it take?"

"Two days."

"Two days? It took over a month for the University to get my visas. How did you do it?"

For the second time that week, I slyly replied, "That is for me to know and for you to find out."

Again, it was none of their business. Besides, a little wonder can do wonders. The mystery was far more potent than the truth because they would wonder, "Whom does Mister John know?" Whatever answer they came up with was going to be better than mine. That worked to my advantage because, more often than not in the UAE, it was not what you knew but whom you knew.

Getting a visa renewed might not sound like much, but the process required navigating layers of bureaucracy, with all the paperwork in Arabic. In addition, most of the clinic staff I dealt with spoke little, if any, English. Getting government paperwork done was not only challenging but could be highly frustrating. And for me, it's not easy to accept help from others, much less depend upon their goodwill.

Nevertheless, the experience of getting my residence visa renewed for the first time changed from negative to positive once I put my trust in two of my former students, Ayesha and Alia. What they did was no small favor, not to me anyway, so I wanted to reward them for helping me more than they probably realized.

"Can I just give you the 500 dirhams? I was going to have to pay it anyway."

"No, Mister John."

"But I want to do something to show my appreciation."

"OK… you please make us your special chocolate cake. And you make it only for us. This time, we do not want to share with anyone!"

"OK, ladies, I will make "The Cake" for you tonight. Come by my office tomorrow. I will hide it in my file cabinet, so no one knows I have it."

"Thank you, Mister John."

"Oh, ladies, one more question. What about the writing? Stamped in black, where the postage stamp should be? What does it say?"

"It is done."

088

CLIFFHANGER

Sue thought I was crazy. OK, that line could start several stories, like this one. Crazy because, just 40 years old, she thought I was too young to be looking for a retirement home - a home to retire to. But then she didn't know what I knew - that I wouldn't be long for the world... of work. So, contrary to her opinion, I thought my timing spot-on.

My objective was to find a property close enough to the United Arab Emirates but far enough away that I'd have a place to go on holiday and then later retire to. While I intended to return to the States every summer for the foreseeable future, I also wanted somewhere closer to the UAE for shorter holidays.

Having checked out and ruled out Asian countries such as Sri Lanka, Thailand, and Brunei, and African countries such as Kenya, Morocco, and Tunisia, I was on to Europe, starting with Mediterranean islands - Malta, Crete, Cyprus, and Mallorca. After ruling out those rocks, I started checking out the mainland - Greece, Italy, France, Portugal, and Spain - the country I was stuck on longer than any other.

With four years of high school Spanish, I figured I'd have a head start there since none of the countries had the "courtesy" to speak English. The weather could be nice if I could find property at elevation, one reason why the area on the south face of the Sierra Nevada Mountains appealed to me most. While remote, it wasn't far from civilization in and out of Spain. And with little to no industry and hanging out in the Atlantic, almost, I guessed the air and water there would be clean-er. Then there was the book *Driving Over Lemons*, one expat's story of settling in Andalusia. What he described sounded like my kind of place.

I began looking at websites of area realtors, bookmarking properties I thought worthy of further investigation. By then, Sue'd come around, joining my search for a vacation/retirement home, as we traded links online. With or without Sue's help, if I found a property that piqued my interest, I'd email the realtor for more information, attaching my one-pager outlining what I was looking for. Too many would then send me info for a condo on the coast, next to a golf course, for a million dollars - what they wanted to sell, not what I wanted to buy.

"Didn't read my one-pager, did you?"

One realtor refused to send me any information on his listings, even though the website said, "Email for more information." Instead, he said, "You show up. Everything is selling fast." Uh-huh. Selling fast? There were properties I asked about that were still for sale on his company's website ten years later.

Another thing that caught my attention was the cave houses in that area of Spain, built into the sides of hills or mountains to beat the summer heat. I wasn't sold on living in a cave, but I found the concept intriguing. Why a property I found just northeast of the small town of Almegíjar appealed to me, the one-room wide house fronting a cliff, the back of the house, rock, the front, a typical house with a panoramic view of the expansive valley below. The property also had a spring and a large cistern to help irrigate the small grove of walnut trees on the flat above the house.

Located on the side of a mountain, off a dead-end dirt track, it was rural, with no neighbor in sight. I called the property "Cliffhanger," eventually referring to it as "Cliffy," the familiarity of the name reflecting my affection for it, increasing with each passing day. I'd even devised a renovation plan and a logo, thinking Cliffy was "the one."

Having missed our chance to go to Thailand the year before, what would've been our first vacation together, alone, Sue and I arranged to travel to the south of Spain, meet with Jack (the realtor), and check out Cliffy, along with another property, a bodega, that Sue had found for herself. Spain not only would be the destination for our first vacation together, alone, but also the first place we'd look for property together, even if separately.

We flew from Dubai to London Heathrow, storing as much of our luggage as possible at the airport so we wouldn't have to lug it around during our side trip to Spain. Much to our dismay, staff told us we couldn't leave any food items in storage, even though they were vacuum-packed inside hard shell luggage. This included 22 pounds of Iranian pistachios and just as many pounds, if not more, of Emirati dates, items I brought back every year to share with family and friends.

Fun, fun, fun, we had to repack on the concourse floor outside the baggage storage counter. Packing my specialty, Sue left me to it as she went off looking for food and drink. All but done repacking, I left our bags for only a minute to throw away some trash. Still keeping an eye on them, I noticed security quietly moving in. "These guys are on top of things." So I did an immediate U-turn and returned to our luggage, security backing off just as quietly as they'd begun moving in, like Homer Simpson retreating into the hedges.

Landing in Málaga at the Pablo Ruiz Picasso Airport - we liked that, an airport named for an artist - our journey to a future together had begun, even if we were unaware. To get around, we rented a car at an agency a few blocks from the airport, a white Renault, and, like most vehicles in Europe then, one with a manual transmission. Why Sue was behind the wheel, except for a short stretch, so I too could have a turn driving over lemons. In places, there were so many on the road that they were unavoidable... <SQUISH SQUISH>

In Málaga, we found a familiar Carrefour, the French megastore with franchises in the UAE. There were some differences, however, as the store in Málaga had pork, one entire aisle - some refrigerated, some cured. I'd never seen so many, and so many kinds of sausage, as I walked around repeating "Snausages!" from an ad for dog treats of the same name.

Sue could've walked away at any time... but didn't. Keeper.

And there was alcohol, two, two aisles of alcohol. Not that I drank a lot, or even a little, but Sue just stood there, admiring the quantity and the price, far less than liquor cost in the UAE, alcohol heavily taxed and only available, legally, for carryout at licensed liquor stores, with a license.

Driving around and then out of Málaga, we saw everything we looked for. While not right where we'd be living, they'd be within an easy enough drive - such as a proper hardware store featuring an entire wall of toilets to choose from.   We also saw what we didn't want - the overrun southern coast. A developer's dream, there were clay tile roofs as far as our eyes could see, but it was not for us, and now we had confirmation.

Just in time for our trip to Spain, the dollar began sliding against the Euro.   We thought it expensive at $1.18 when we arrived, but by the time we returned to the UAE later that summer, a Euro cost $1.40, so no Spain. Just too expensive. Just as well because a change in government, brought about by the 2004 Madrid commuter train bombings (3/11), resulted in new laws designed to limit developers along that overrun southern coast.

While it was not their intended purpose, those laws severely limited what owners could do renovating in rural areas, essentially destroying the market for mountain properties like Cliffy, the main reason why those I asked about were still for sale on that realtor's website ten years later.   Cliffy needed "mucho worko," but with the new restrictions, my renovation plan would've been all but impossible to carry out.

Cliffy could've been something, but it was not to be. It was not "the one." There were other concerns, such as maybe not having enough water, a problem that would've worsened as Spain suffered years of drought following our visit. A 2023 check of Cliffy on Google Earth showed a property noticeably browner than when we were there, and it appeared the walnut grove had died, all the trees gone. Maybe the spring dried up, and the cistern size wouldn't have mattered without water.

A local water bottler, Lanjarón, named for the town where they extracted their product, was still in business. They bottled the best water I ever drank.   I was so impressed that I even exported a few bottles.   Yes, I went to Spain and brought back, amongst other things, water.   At least the customs inspectors in the States didn't confiscate it, as they did my Spanish sausages. Canadian inspectors also confiscated Sue's sausages. Pistachios, OK. Dates, OK. Water, OK. Sausages… snatched.

Disappointed Cliffy and then Spain didn't work out, Sue and I would return anytime to visit.   We enjoyed our stay in Bubión, the middle child of three whitewashed villages, Capileira and Pampaneira, the others. The weather was great, the scenery gorgeous, and the food tasty… when we were served. Because the first restaurant we tried in Bubión… I can't say they wouldn't serve us because they would've first had to acknowledge our existence to deny service. They didn't. We sat there for an hour, doing everything we could to attract attention, short of clocking a server. Nothing.

Taking the hint, we got up and walked across the narrow street to another restaurant. The wait staff there was more than happy to serve us, every night, for three nights.   Sitting at a street-side table, in addition to sampling the tapas, I ate the same pork dish three nights in a row. It was that good. Ignored in the first place, in the second, not only did the staff give us service with a smile, a black cat joined us (me), sitting in my lap for every meal, sensing, correctly, he'd found a friend (sucker).

We stayed at a B&B with a view of the valley. Gorgeous in the daytime, the valley held a certain fascination, even in the dark.   We walked up to a lookout bench every night after dinner to watch the sunset, then gaze into the eventual inky darkness except for the headlights of cars winding their way home, including one near the top of the mountain on the opposite side of the valley.

"There's a road up there?"

Shortly after the headlights went off, a porch light went on, and stayed on, a single light at the top of a mountain. Every night we were there, we watched someone drive home in the dark, except for their vehicle's headlights, then turn on their porch light once they arrived. We called the home we couldn't see, "Casa de Pepe."

The property search didn't work out for Sue either, as she didn't even have a chance to inspect hers. The realtor informed her upon our arrival that "It just sold." I thought that a good thing, though, hoping Sue would "get with the program" and start looking with me, and maybe she was hoping I'd do the same and start looking with her, so we'd be looking for the same property, for one dream come true, not two.

But after that trip, the first Sue and I ever took together, alone, it happened. It was no longer "she" looking and "I" looking, but "we" looking, which might've had something to do with the Bubión B&B's bed… broken.

"We found it like that."

But we didn't.

089

TIME TRAVEL

When I lived in the United Arab Emirates, where every day was not a holiday, except at the American embassy (expat joke), my birthday stretched over two days. "Say what?" said Sue, she new to my take on such things, we only just having found each other and each other's company pleasant. So I explained…

"I was born at 10:56 pm. Because the UAE is nine hours ahead of where I was born, my "odometer" doesn't roll over until 7:56 am the day after my birthday. So I have a two-day birthday - the date of my birth, September 2, and the day I become a full year older, September 3."

That's when I first noticed Sue shakes her head a lot. Yes, she does.

After we moved to Ecuador and my birthday approached, Sue reminded me we were living in the same time zone in which I was born, so my birthday would no longer be a two-day deal, just one. No longer would I be entitled to an extra day's dispensation, not that she ever thought I was in the UAE.

However, thanks to social media, the day before the day, I received Happy Birthday wishes from friends and former Dubai Women's College colleagues living in

Australia, where, for half the day, it was already tomorrow and my birthday.

"Yes! Two days! I'm the birthday boy!"

Sue shakes her head a lot. Yes, she does.

Two-day birthday? While Sue was adamant that wasn't a thing, it was nothing compared to how I manipulated time in 2017, the day before my birthday, when I traveled back in time. Sure, many people do that on their birthday, to be 29 years old again, but I'm not one of those people. That day, I was what I was, or was about to be, 55 years old.

For that birthday, I juggled the time even more than usual, an impossible solution necessary for an impossible problem. Because, according to Apple, the issue with my computer didn't exist, couldn't exist. Nevertheless, it did, and still did after four hours of head-banging, searching for a solution.

Shocking, I know, but Apple's online customer support, fiendishly designed only to handle problems that existed, was of absolutely no help. Throw in that I was living off a dead-end dirt (we aspired to gravel) road on the side of a mountain in a remote part of southern Ecuador, and I could only generate one response from Apple...

"Take your computer in for service."

"My computer isn't broken, Apple is!"

"Would you like to talk to a real person?"

"Sure!"

"Please submit a serial number for the product in question."

"Apple doesn't have a serial number!"

And when I submitted my computer's serial number because... what else could I do?

"Take your computer in for service."

"ARGH!"

No matter what I tried, I couldn't escape the "Take your computer in for service" black hole.

"MY COMPUTER ISN'T WHAT'S BROKEN!"

All I wanted was to upgrade my operating system. One level. One. Apple, for reasons known only to Apple, prevents customers from accessing old operating system files because… that would be helpful. Knowing this, I'd been downloading each new OS, even if I didn't immediately use it, as legitimate copies are almost impossible to come by once Apple releases a new one, and I never knew when I might need an old one. I was on top of the situation, yet the first time I tried to upgrade using one of those archived OS installers, my current OS informed me the file was either corrupt or tampered with, blocking it from launching.

"SONOFABITCH!"

If I couldn't find a solution, my only options were not to upgrade or upgrade to the latest OS. What Apple wanted, what I wanted, irrelevant. I didn't want to because upgrading to the latest OS would've required me to upgrade some pricey application software, including one requiring a subscription service.

"Sorry, our subscription service isn't available off your dead-end dirt (you aspire to gravel) road. Please move to a different location."

Four hours in, out of ideas, and almost out of patience, I took one last stab at a Google search for a solution to my problem because I am just that stubborn - a donkey once named after me. Serious - John the Donkey. My persistence paid off, though, because there it was, detailed in some obscure tech-head magazine article, my problem, and better still, a solution.

All App Store apps require an Apple Worldwide Developer Relations Intermediate Certificate, including operating system installers. These certificates enable the user's current operating system to verify an app, confirming that no attacker, hacker, or nefarious Nigerian prince has corrupted or modified the file. Searching Apple Support for reasons my OS installer wouldn't install, I found no mention of these certificates.

Thanks, Apple. As a customer since 1988, you were once a lovable little company, one I defended back in 1998 when all my Windows-using friends and colleagues mocked my Mac and me, proclaiming, "Apple will be out of business before you need a new computer!" These were the same people who spent their weekends working on their PCs to get them working while I worked on my Mac because it always worked the way I wanted it to.

Almost always, because on September 1, 2018, when I attempted to upgrade with the archived installer, my OS blocked it from launching because its certificate expired on February 14, 2016, but kept this information to itself. One of the things I find frustrating about computers is that when they don't work as expected, they rarely explain why. Instead, they sit there, taunting me with their silent but oh so heard ditty, "I know something I won't tell, I won't tell, I won't tell, I know something I won't tell... so you can go to hell."

Knowing why my installer wouldn't launch and how to make it do so, I felt like The Great and Powerful Oz. To workaround the expired certificate, I only needed to travel back in time by shutting off the "Set date and time automatically" feature and then changing the date on my computer to February 13, 2016. With my Mac not knowing what day it was, what day it really was, the expired certificate on my archived OS installer no longer was.

"Wallah!" I upgraded my operating system, and it only took a few minutes… and four hours… and a year off my life because, according to my computer, in those few minutes, I went from 54 years old to 53, then back to 54. Then, the next day, my birthday, I turned 55. Like Mr. Peabody and his boy, Sherman, if only I had a real Wayback Machine.

I was happy, though, with not only my upgraded operating system but also that I knew more than I did the day or year before - such head-banging experiences how I learned almost everything I know about computers. Why, after completing the upgrade in far less time than it took to understand why I couldn't and then how I could, I wanted to thank the post's author for his help…

"Sorry. Comments for this article are now closed."

090

RIDING SHOTGUN WITH GUS

"Red light!" Gus would stop. "Green Light!" Gus would go. Were we playing the popular children's game? Nope, just cruising the mean streets of Dubai in Gus' car, me riding shotgun.

After we moved to Al Ain in the summer of 1991, a colleague, Gus, and I acquired new cars. In an attempt to save money, he bought a Russian-built Lada. If you're unfamiliar with the brand, AvtoVAZ manufactures them in Tolyatti, Samara Oblast. Yes, Tolyatti, Samara Oblast. Apparently, it's the Detroit, Michigan of Russia.

Ladas were cheap, around $6000 for a brand-new sedan. There was also a Lada SUV, jokingly marketed as being able to hold more passengers… who could get out and push when it inevitably broke down. While the sedan was nothing much to look at, the supposedly better-built SUV had an appealing quirkiness about it.

Neither selling point would dissuade me from buying the cheapest Honda, a Civic DX, for just $9000. At first, Gus was quite proud he'd saved $3000 compared to what I paid for my Honda. And in his mind, and only his, there was a certain cool factor about driving around in a Russian car.

Until reality set in. Bare bones transportation, his Lada didn't have a radio. Some would say it didn't have an engine, as Gus' car had trouble climbing the desert dunes under the highway between Al Ain and Dubai. Riding along, it felt like that long, slow climb up the first incline on a roller coaster, except in Gus' Lada, I was never sure we would make it over the top.

Neither was Gus, even after he switched off the air conditioner before beginning an ascent. As for our comfort, or lack thereof, whether the A/C was on or off didn't matter because it didn't cool the air - it just sucked what little engine power there was while trying and failing to do so. Who needed air conditioning in the desert between Al Ain and Dubai anyway?

At least Gus and his passengers could roll down the windows… until the mechanisms broke, as his Lada started falling apart almost immediately after he drove it off the dealer's lot. So, in case anyone was wondering why Gus wedged his used matchbooks in strategic points around the car's interior, it was his feeble attempt to eliminate rattles.

Probably why Gus eventually stopped asking me, "Enjoying your $3000 radio?"

Instead, he'd call and ask, "Mister John, you up for a trip to Dubai?"

"Sure!"

"…wanna drive?"

"Sure."

And I didn't mind because I had a radio, a tape deck, and air conditioning that worked great even when climbing a dune at 90 mph. My Honda was a great little car, one I knew, and Gus knew, would get us there and back, one that never cost me a dirham in repairs.

Well, there was that one time a patch of paint required some buffing after a UAE University student,

"Crazy Badria," wrote "I Love You" on the driver's side door... in blood... hers... that the sun then baked into the finish. It was good for me that trying to write a message in blood on a vertical surface during a scorching hot afternoon resulted in a message no one could read, including me.

Indecipherable, I assumed the message was "written" in Arabic until Badria set me straight. Good thing because if "I Love You" had been legible and seen by the wrong person - on the UAEU campus, that would've been most everyone - her love note could've made a significant problem for me - a get fired, get deported, return to the States, unemployed, kind of problem.

Before returning to the States, voluntarily, Gus somehow got three years out of his Lada, selling his marvel of Russian engineering to an older married couple, Gordon and Barbara, colleagues of ours, for $1500. It wasn't worth half that, probably why all I ever heard about Gus' old Lada were complaints, as I shared an office with Gordon and Barbara until the building burned to the ground - another story for another book.

But when the Lada belonged to Gus, as if driving or pushing it wasn't difficult enough, as if driving in the UAE wasn't dangerous enough, Gus was colorblind. As I understand it, those with color blindness can still see colors, but they often appear washed out. Red is brown, purple and blue look the same, pinkish-colored people appear sickly greenish-yellow, and, if you're a fan of the Dr. Suess book *Green Eggs and Ham*, peanut butter looks green.

It's more common than I thought, as 1 in 12 men and 1 in 200 women have the inherited genetic condition based on the X chromosome. Women with the gene aren't color blind but have a 50% chance of passing it to their sons. A colorblind man can't pass the gene to his son, but his daughters become carriers. Fewer women are color blind because their father must be color blind and their mother a carrier, and even then, there's only a 50% chance.

As Gus explained it, the two stop-and-go lights that mattered most were just shades of gray, which made me wonder why, when most colorblind people are red/green colorblind, those two lights were red and green. Whose idea was that? Not someone who ever rode shotgun around Dubai in a Russian-built car with a red/green colorblind driver, that's for sure.

In roundabout-happy Al Ain, so few traffic lights, Gus' red/green color blindness wasn't an issue. The same could not be said when he drove in Dubai, where intersections with traffic lights were far more common. When he could still drive his Lada to Dubai with some hope that the car would make it back to Al Ain on its own and not on the flatbed of a recovery truck, Gus was happy to have someone riding shotgun, someone to call out the color of oncoming stop-and-go lights.

He was even more grateful when first in the queue, waiting for the lights to change. There's already enough pressure, with impatient drivers tailing behind, even when red and green aren't two shades of gray. I asked what he did in such situations when he was driving alone.

"I just wait for some asshole behind me to start honking their horn."

In the UAE, drivers in the queue started honking their horns before, before the lights changed in anticipation that they soon would.

So next time you're behind a car at the head of the line that doesn't immediately punch it when the light goes green, the driver might not be waiting for a particular shade of green, staring at their smartphone, trying to find first gear, taking a swig of beer, or even daydreaming. They might, might be colorblind, with no one riding shotgun to call out, "Green light!"

091

I STILL HAVE TEN FINGERS

Having eaten off a stainless steel plate for years, I have some understanding of how the one inside my Grandpa Curran's head contributed to his issues. His plate patched his skull, necessary after Grandpa took a nasty fall years before I was born. When I was old enough to understand, Grandma told me doctors at the Mayo Clinic told her that even if Grandpa somehow survived emergency brain surgery, he'd likely be a vegetable for the rest of his life. Doctors, even at the Mayo Clinic, can be wrong. Fortunately, they were, or this story would be a different one.

The reason Grandma told me about Grandpa's operation was because I needed to know… what to do when he had a grand mal seizure. A byproduct of his brain surgery and the metal plate, it was not a matter of if but when one would occur. When it did, there was little anyone could do, even a doctor, other than keeping Grandpa from hurting himself, which included getting a tongue depressor into his mouth to prevent him from biting and/or swallowing his tongue.

Having bitten my tongue a few times, I got that. What I didn't get was how anyone could swallow their tongue… because I tried. Even though it was already in my mouth and halfway down my throat, I just couldn't do it, deciding it must be one of those things only grown-ups did, like drinking cola.

While there was something amiss inside Grandpa's head, he was among the most knowledgeable people I've ever known. A voracious reader, there were always stacks of books around his home, not just to impress the guests who rarely dropped by. Many a Friday night, I was in tow as Grandma ran errands after dropping Grandpa off at the Eau Claire Public Library so he could exchange the previous week's reading for the next.

While the plate in his head helped explain some of Grandpa's behavior, it wasn't his only problem. A chemist at Uniroyal Tire, long-term exposure to toxic chemicals forced him to retire early, on disability. Unable to drive a car because of the seizures and living in the woods off a dead-end (paved) road, he didn't get out much. Perhaps that is why he made a point to keep up on current events, as, in addition to books, he also read newspapers and magazines, especially since he had no use for the TV, or as he called it, "The Idiot Box."

Every town has that one guy who is always writing letters to the editor, and in Eau Claire, that man was my Grandpa Curran. Not some nut with a mailbox, his letters to the editor were often published, not just in the local newspaper but also in national publications. Even though family and friends didn't always appreciate Grandpa's pointed remarks - acid often the only moisture in his otherwise desert-dry sense of humor - newspaper and magazine editors did. Why I smiled the first time one of my Letters to the Editor was published in a national periodical (*Architectural Record* magazine), knowing how proud Grandpa would've been, especially with my post containing just the right amount of snark. I think.

A perpetual fidgeter, no doubt owing to his brain surgery and resulting metal plate, and given his propensity for speaking his mind, Grandpa made those around him uncomfortable. Why few others other than editors liked him. Even as a kid, I could tell, although out of politeness, most at least left some doubt. Grandpa, on the other hand, left no doubt. I can't say with certainty, but I think Grandpa knew exactly what he was doing - filtering the herd.

Despite his gruff exterior, I liked Grandpa, and I know he liked me, so I seldom saw the cranky old man I'm sure most others did and probably didn't much care for. But then Grandpa seemed to like dogs more than most people. Probably because dogs didn't say stupid things or do stupid things, mostly, or bring drama to his door unless they had an unfortunate encounter with a skunk, a car, or another dog. And they generally liked people, even Grandpa.

Given all he taught me, I have no doubt he would've made a great teacher… if he didn't have to deal with a classroom full of people, especially the stupid ones. I think my learning what he had to teach was important to him, and why the patience he rarely displayed with others he had with me.

Like when he helped teach me to read. He was never so patient until the day came when he said, "You don't need me anymore. You know how to read." He was right. I did know how to read. I just liked reading with Grandpa even though I no longer needed his help. It was time to move on and learn other things, like stacking firewood, because life wasn't all about fancy book learning.

As a young man, Grandpa worked as a lumberjack and later as a tree buyer for Nekoosa Paper, so he had a seemingly endless supply of lessons to teach me about the woods he lived in and loved. Having only recently learned to read, I wasn't old enough to chop firewood. Instead, I picked up the pieces resulting from Grandpa's deftly swung axe. He stressed the importance of carefully stacking firewood so it wouldn't topple. I don't know if it was my spatial abilities or ones developed helping him, but my stacks were always tightly packed, even as I piled firewood higher than me.

When came the day he decided I was old enough to swing his axe, he taught me how and how to do it safely. To emphasize his "safety first" philosophy, Grandpa told me the story of a young man he once worked with who was having trouble splitting a log that just wouldn't sit still. So he propped it up lengthwise, holding it in place with the sole of his boot. That young man split the log all right, along with his boot and foot within.

"He didn't think it through, boy," Grandpa said with a chuckle.

More of a show me than tell me teacher, Grandpa liked graphic examples, probably because they saved him from having to talk so much. His lessons taught me another lesson, useful for when I became a teacher - make learning memorable and students will remember. Like the day he decided I was old enough to learn how to use a lawn mower.

That lesson took place in his front yard under a large white pine tree and Grandma's watchful eye as she peered out the window above the kitchen sink. Using a sturdy stick, Grandpa pointed out where to put the oil, stressing why the engine should never run out of that. He pointed out the cap to the gas tank, telling me it was OK if the mower ran out of gas, but I should let the engine cool some before refilling the tank.

"That's a good time to get a drink of water, son."

After showing me the proper setting for the choke to get the Briggs & Stratton started, he pulled the cord a few times before the mower roared to life. An angry little machine, it spit out remnants from the previous mow and whatever wasn't tight to the ground under the spinning blade, my bare shins peppered with debris.

Above the din of the two-stroke engine, Grandpa shouted, "THAT'S WHY YOU WEAR PANTS WHEN YOU'RE MOWING, BOY. NOT SHORTS."

But the lesson wasn't over just yet. Grandpa then handed me the stick.

"YOU WOULDN'T WANT ME TO HIT YOU WITH THIS STICK, WOULD YOU, BOY?"

"NO."

"WHY NOT?"

"IT WOULD HURT."

"WHY?"

"BECAUSE IT'S HARD."

Grandpa then took the stick from my hands and jammed it into the opening, where the mower expelled the cut grass. While the mower protested some, the blade never stopped spinning. After a few seconds, Grandpa removed the stick… what was left of it.

"SEE WHAT HAPPENED TO THIS STICK, BOY?"

"YES."

"THINK YOUR HAND WOULD FARE ANY BETTER?"

"NO."

"THEN DON'T PUT YOUR HAND INSIDE THE MOWER. OK?"

"OK."

"WHY?"

"BECAUSE I DON'T WANT MY HAND TO END UP LIKE THAT STICK."

Another valuable teaching lesson learned - always check for understanding.

Having determined he'd gotten his point across, Grandpa Curran walked away, leaving me to the mowing. We never talked about lawnmower safety again. Didn't need to. Point made. Lesson learned. Why I still have ten fingers.

092

440 PESOS!

"What are you doing?" the county sheriff's deputy asked as he shined his flashlight in our faces.

"Ummm… unloading luggage?"

"Whose luggage?"

"Mine!" anxious to get my imported treasures from Mexico into our house.

"This is our son. He just returned from a school trip to Mexico," Del interjected.

After a few more quick flicks off his flashlight across our faces and then over the contents of the car's trunk, the deputy seemed satisfied we weren't involved in the commotion next door that got him called out at one in the morning.

"Sorry to bother you. Have a good evening," he said before returning his attention to our neighbors.

Years before cable TV came to our home, those neighbors were our pay-per-view channel, seemingly providing an R-rated show every Saturday night. The actors weren't so good, but each week, the plot thickened, often bringing new storylines and sometimes new characters - life on low-rent Lawson Drive.

After getting my bags inside, following a flight from Mexico City to Chicago and a school bus ride to

Waupaca, I was pleased to discover my Mexican treasure was still in 33 pieces, including the board. I'd always admired the marble chess set Jay picked up when he was in Italy, so when I saw an opportunity to buy one of my own, I did.

As I unwrapped the pieces and carefully placed them on the board, I saw Ma adding up the cost and not liking the mounting subtotal. Del grew uneasy as well, but I think for a different reason, perhaps concerned he'd suffer collateral damage when Ma finally blew a gasket. So before she could explode, I figured I'd better start my sales pitch.

"It's marble!"

"I swapped pieces from two other sets to get just the one I wanted."

"I haggled for half an hour to get the best price!"

"Nice, huh?"

It was all true. It was all marble, and negotiations at the market in Mexico City began with what exactly it was I wanted to buy, "I want this board, these white pieces, and those black pieces," pointing to three different sets on three different shelves on three different aisles.

"No problemo."

After all the pieces I wanted were arranged for my approval on the board I wanted, the real bargaining began. Thirty minutes of haggling later, the last ten to narrow the 100-peso gap between his final price and my final offer, each side was happy enough that the sale was made.

I probably could've done better, but it was my last day in Mexico City and Mexico. Just a few hours from heading to the airport for a flight to Chicago, I didn't have time to hold out for an even better deal. Besides, it was the set I wanted after swapping boards and pieces.

With my suitcase already packed and loaded on the bus for the ride to the airport, the chess set would make the trip home in my carry-on bag. Wrapped in newspaper, the pieces filled the bottom of my bag while the board, also wrapped in the day's headlines, fitted only on the diagonal. Even then, I couldn't close the bag as the board stuck out the top.

It was the only souvenir I wanted to bring back from Mexico. Had I known we'd move to a house with trees in the yard the following year, I would've also brought back a few hammocks. And those colorful Mexican blankets? For years, I wished I'd bought more than the two I did. But it left me with a reason to return or move to the UAE or Ecuador, where I could purchase more "exotic" blankets.

But I was beginning to wish I hadn't bought even the one marble chess set, what with Ma glaring at it and me. Unable to listen to my sales pitch one second more, in a tone that told me any answer was going to be the wrong one, she blurted out, "How much did you pay for this!"

"440 pesos!" I replied with as much pride and confidence as I could muster, given the lateness of the hour and the longness of my day.

"440 pesos!" she gasped as if I'd mortgaged the family's future. "How much is that?"

"About 22 dollars."

"22 dollars! How come you didn't buy two?"

093

DEBBIE DOES PLATTEVILLE

In the summer of 1975, a not-quite 13-year-old version of me wanted to see the blockbuster movie *Jaws*. If you've not seen it, let me explain the plot... There's this killer great white shark and this not-so-great great white shark hunter who's told, "You're gonna need a bigger boat." With no nudity, no more cursing than I heard at home, and not much blood and guts for a movie about a killer shark, the Motion Picture Association rated *Jaws* PG (Parental Guidance Suggested), so I could've seen it.

But didn't because Ma forbid it after hearing of those who'd seen the movie and were then afraid to go swimming in Lake Altoona, a 720-acre manmade body of water just east of Eau Claire, Wisconsin, about as far as one can get from an ocean and still be in North America. Afraid to go swimming? In Lake Altoona? After watching a movie about shark attacks? Off fictional Amity Island? In the Atlantic Ocean? For fuck's sake... I wish I'd known that expression then.

Despite Ma's ban, I still tried maneuvering my way into seeing *Jaws* on movie night with Jay. Cruising down State Street hill in his '65 Mustang - Caspian blue, white convertible top, baby moon hubcaps - Jay asked, "What theater are we going to?" I told him which one, just not that *Jaws* was playing there, hoping he'd let me see it, payback for all the times I saved him from a stern talking to. Just turned 20, Jay wasn't my parent or guardian, but he was an adult, sort of, so he could've made that command decision.

Approaching the theater, he saw the marquee - "JAWS." "Your mother said you're not allowed to see that." Jay didn't have a problem with me seeing the movie but knew he'd have one with Ma if she ever discovered I did on his watch. So he drove a few blocks further, and that night, we saw Disney's *The Apple Dumpling Gang*. If you've not seen it, let me explain the plot... Don Knotts and Tim Conway, two of my favorites, did what they did best. It was a delightful movie, just not the one I wanted to see.

It'd be years before I'd see *Jaws*, on a small screen. While the shark wasn't nearly what it would've been on the big screen, I saw it several times up close and personal during the tram ride (sit on the right) at Universal Studios Hollywood. I thought the mechanical shark was more goofy than scary, what with its toothy grin and googly eyes, why I wasn't afraid to go swimming afterward, and wouldn't have been when I was not quite 13 either... BECAUSE I HAD A FUNCTIONING BRAIN! Even if you didn't, I heard Lewis Black voicing those last words.

During my eight months in Florida, because I didn't want to live there nine, there were multiple shark attacks, one causing a young couple to split the hard way. Why, when I day tripped to a nearby beach a short time later, I didn't go swimming, just walked out a ways, no more than knee deep, on the lookout for fins, listening for tuba music... "duunnn dunnn... duuuunnnn duun... duuunnnnnnnnn dun dun dun dun dun dun dun dun dun dun dunnnnnnnnnnnn dunnnn…" Respect… WHERE AND WHEN IT WAS NECESSARY! Again, even if you didn't, I heard Lewis Black voicing those last words.

Jay and I saw the darkened insides of Eau Claire's three downtown theaters many times over the nine summers I spent there after Ma and I moved to Waupaca in 1971. There was another, though, over on Water Street, I never saw the inside of - the West End Ice Cream Parlor & Studio West Movie House. Across the Chippewa River from the bulk of the University of Wisconsin-Eau Claire campus, Water Street, just nine blocks long, was lined with several businesses catering to students, including the bike shop on the 400-block where Ma and Del bought my first and only ten-speed, a birthday present.

Studio West stood in the 200-block, an ice cream parlor fronting the narrow but deep one-story building. Along a long hallway leading to the theater in the back was a Nazi memorabilia display… as there always is. During the day, the theater screened classic comedies featuring The Marx Brothers, Abbott & Costello, The Three Stooges, and the like, but after dark… porn flicks, such as *Deep Throat* and *Behind The Green Door*. Perhaps why family and friends never mentioned Studio West. By the time I was old enough to know what no one was talking about, I no longer lived in Eau Claire, even part-time.

After moving to Waupaca full-time, I didn't live there for a year before I was off to the University of Florida, then transferred to the University of Wisconsin-Platteville the following year. Located 20 or so miles northeast of Dubuque, Iowa, UWP was the epitome of a "suitcase college." In case you're not familiar with the term, let me explain… The vast majority of students went home for the weekend.

With no vehicle and no particular place to go anyway, I was almost always one of the remaining few, my dorm wing of 35 often down to single digits on weekends. Always looking for something to do, if we couldn't find something on campus, we ventured off campus, like the Friday night we went to see the only movie I ever would at Platteville's only theater. I think every male, and maybe every female remaining on campus, was there that weekend, along with a horde of townsfolk, the theater standing room only.

If she could've, Ma would've forbidden my seeing that movie too, but I was going on 21, not 13, and besides, "Everyone else is going to see *Debbie Does Dallas 2!* the iconic sequel to the iconic original. If you've not seen either, let me explain the plots… The first documented the fundraising efforts of Debbie and her friends, as Debbie needed money to travel to Dallas, aspiring to be a Cowboys Cheerleader. The sequel documented her adventures as she made her way to Dallas. The titles were misleading, though, as Debbie didn't "do" Dallas in either movie, but rest assured, she did "do" …things.

Before that night, I'd never seen an X-rated movie, so I had no idea what to expect… other than the obvious. But then, back then, the screening of an X-rated feature film in the sleepy farming community's theater was unexpected, and so too was the behavior of moviegoers, who turned out to be a free sideshow.

There was the older married couple across the aisle, the husband's repeated marveling at the "outstanding talent" of one of the actors, and his wife's repeated pleas to "Shush." There was Crazy Joe, a late twenty-something Navy veteran who lived on my wing, voicing hilarious sound effects, including a perfectly timed impression of a boot being pulled from muck. It wasn't just these isolated incidents, as the audience turned interactive, vocally, not only contributing commentary but also chants, cheers, and even a few boos, appropriate, I thought, for a movie about a cheerleader.

Despite the good time had by all, *Debbie Does Dallas 2* would be the last such movie I'd see, in a theater - been there, done that, got the story, don't need a repeat, same as it was for the double public execution I witnessed in Al Ain.   Yup, in the United Arab Emirates, a conservative Muslim country where too much cleavage on a magazine cover drew a censor's big black magic marker, I had a front-row seat to a government-sanctioned double death by firing squad...

"You are looking live at the Al Ain Prison Execution Grounds, where today, one Emirati and one Iranian will meet their maker.   Hello everybody, I'm Brent Musburger..."

During my first year in the UAE, new to Muslim countries and extreme government censorship, I asked the Egyptian and Muslim girlfriend I didn't have - because having would've violated some rules - if she'd ever seen the nudity banned in the UAE and her home country.   With an intriguing mix of pride and shame, she admitted she and some friends once got hold of a Playboy magazine.

"And?..."

"The women... they were all so... look at me," she voicing those last three words in an unintentional but spot-on impression of a sultry Lauren Bacall.   I got a good laugh out of that remark, more for how she said than what she said, in a conversation I never thought I'd have with a Muslim woman.   Given her way with words, even in her second language, I can only imagine what she would've said about *Debbie Does Dallas 2* had she seen the movie.   She had not.

Owing to such extreme censorship, typical of almost every country for two thousand miles in every direction, when the UAE's Ministry of Information & Culture announced it would permit local theaters to screen the movie *Basic Instinct*, the anticipation was palpable. So, too, was the disappointment when the film, cut to 46 minutes, failed to deliver. If you've not seen *Basic Instinct*, all of it, let me explain the plot… An attractive woman uncrosses and then crosses her legs.

Knowing better, I didn't pay to watch what was left of the movie, but others did, left to wonder, "What was all the fuss about?"

"Did you think the UAE government would permit what made *Basic Instinct Basic Instinct* to be shown in theaters here? For fuck's sake…" By then, I knowing that expression.

In a country that banned public displays of affection, even between husband and wife, prostitution, as you might expect, was also illegal. Yet, Dubai had whorehouses, out in the open if one knew where to look. Nevertheless, the police rarely arrested anyone for the crime because a conviction required four males to witness any sexual encounter, and how often does that happen? Even Debbie didn't have that many… in the movie anyway.

094

SPEED THRILLS

The "Theory of Relativity." That's what I used to judge my speed when cruising city streets, seeing how my bicycle didn't have a speedometer. If cars were passing me, I was going slow. If I was keeping up, I was going. If I was passing cars, I was going fast.

I never wore a helmet, either. The days when bicycles were my primary mode of transportation were long over before helmets became something conscientious cyclists wore. But then, if bicycles were a new invention, they'd be outlawed, helmet or not - just too dangerous.

Not that it would matter much since I don't see so many kids riding bikes anymore, smartphones now taking them wherever they want to go. When I was a kid, our home telephone was a Ma Bell special, any color my Ma wanted, as long as it was black, but since she couldn't afford long distance, I couldn't get far on the phone.

I couldn't have cared less because my bike allowed me to go anywhere my legs could pedal when I lived on Eau Claire's north side. Some days, it was north to the cemetery and Dells Pond. Some days, it was east to the base of Mount Tom and Gustafson's ice cream store.

Some days, it was west to the Sterling Pulp and Paper mill and the dam on the Chippewa River. I didn't need an adult to get me where I was going because my bike could take me there as long as I was home before dinner or dark, whichever came first. And back then, nobody looked twice at an eight-year-old boy riding a bike by himself - except for that creepy guy who lived around the corner.

My bike was a blue Schwinn Sting-Ray, with butterfly handlebars, metallic white banana seat, 20-inch tires - the back a two-and-a-half-inch wide slick, and no fenders because "Fenders are for girls!" The only way it could've looked faster was if it'd been painted red. The only way it could've gone faster was if it had gears, but it did not. My bike was a one-speed - my speed.

Unless... I used gravity to help me go faster, which I did on the days that took me south to downtown Eau Claire because downtown really was down, situated in a bowl at the confluence of the Eau Claire and Chippewa Rivers. The easiest way to get downtown from our apartment on the north side was via Putnam Street, past The Alibi, a corner bar at the top of the hill. Known for its roast beef sandwiches, The Alibi was a popular after-work destination for the many factory workers in the neighborhood.

At the bottom of the hill was a rail yard. Across the tracks on the right was the Bunny Bread bakery. It always smelled so good. The blocks-long Uniroyal Tire factory was on the left, where Grandpa Curran, Uncle Mike, and Susie's Bob worked. It always smelled... After that, just a few more zigs and zags, and I was downtown.

Even though Ma and I moved to Waupaca just before my ninth birthday, Del still lived in Eau Claire full-time. So for the next nine summers, Ma and I lived there too, my bike moving with me, even though it took up too much trunk space, even after disassembling.

The first of those nine summers, we lived on the north side, in the same neighborhood we moved from. The second, we lived down in the bowl, downtown. For the last seven, we lived on the south side, above the bowl, just blocks from the upper campus of the University of Wisconsin-Eau Claire and a ride down the Garfield Avenue hill to the lower campus, sandwiched between the drop-off and the Chippewa River.

While many hilly streets led to downtown Eau Claire, Garfield Avenue was the most exhilarating to go down on a bicycle. With a sweeping right-hand curve from top to bottom, the street was so steep that the city often closed it to traffic in the winter, as any amount of snow or ice made it impossible to go up and impossible not to go down. Garfield Avenue wasn't the busiest of streets, even when road conditions were good. Most of the traffic on the hill was the pedestrian kind - university students huffing and puffing their way up or trying to keep from falling head-over-heels on their way down.

Living in Eau Claire just for the summer, I didn't have any friends in what was my old hometown, so most days, I had to make fun. When we lived on the south side, making fun often included riding my bike down Garfield Hill, just for the thrill, something I'd done many times without incident until...

Already whizzing down the hill at a coed-impressing speed (even though I did not yet understand why that mattered), I reversed the pedals to slow myself because to go down Garfield Hill at full speed was suicidal. Much to my dismay, the pedals offered no resistance to my backpedaling.

Looking down, I saw my bicycle chain, broken, dragging on the asphalt.

"Uh-oh."

With no brakes and already going too fast to stop myself with my feet, I realized I was about to go down Garfield Hill at full speed... something no one in their right mind would ever do. Waiting for me at the bottom on the right was a side road T-boning Garfield Avenue and, at high speed, a too-tight turn, so crashing into pedestrians, cross traffic, or oncoming traffic were all definite possibilities.

Sure enough, as the intersection came into view, it was full of students, oblivious to the kid careening down the hill on his runaway bike. Why I screamed, "LOOOOOOOK OWWWWWWWT!" loud enough to turn heads... on the other side of the city. While I got their attention, they froze, at first, until those students most likely to get run over finally processed the situation just in time to scatter.

Luckily, there was no oncoming traffic or parked cars, but knowing I was going too fast to hold the curve, I picked a place on the opposite side of the road to crash - a small clearing just to the right of a signpost. Not wanting to find out how far I could fly, I pulled up on my bike just before I would've struck the concrete curb, landing on the narrow patch of grass between the road and the riverbank. No sooner had I hit the grass than I stuck out my left arm to snag the signpost, which I did, just enough to send my bike flying from under me. If not for some scraggly trees on the riverbank, my bike and I would've tumbled down the high bank and into the Chippewa River.

Just like that, my thrill ride down Garfield Hill at full speed was over, some students rushing to the crash site...

"Hey, kid, you OK?"

"Yeah… yeah… I'm OK."

"Oh man, that was so cool! You must've been going a hundred miles an hour!"

Just like that, whatever hurt didn't matter because university students thought what I did was cool. I don't know about 100mph, but I doubt anyone has ever gone down Garfield Hill faster than I did that day and walked away, pushing their bike. Except for the broken chain that started the chain of events, neither my bike nor I suffered enough damage for Ma or Del to notice once I got home. They did, however, ask why I was late for dinner.

"My bike chain broke, so I had to walk home."

Sure, I left out what happened in between, but I saw no sense in telling Ma and Del the whole truth when the truth would do.

095

WHEN I WAS A DICKHEAD

National Basketball Association Hall of Famer and legendary trash-talker Larry Bird won the league's inaugural 3-Point Shooting Contest in 1986. Before the 1987 contest, Bird walked into the locker room and told his fellow competitors, "I'm winning this." And he did, raising his index finger before his final shot hit nothing but net. With typical Bird gamesmanship, he hadn't even bothered to remove his warm-up jacket. He had little to say the following year because, as he explained, "We all know who's going to win." And he did.

When it came to quiz nights in Al Ain, our team couldn't compete with Bird's talent for trash-talking opponents, but the other quiz teams knew they, too, were likely playing for second place because, in our first season of competition, we won an astounding 21 times. Our team's first quiz night was at the InterContinental Hotel's Horse and Jockey Pub, an acceptable reproduction of a typical English pub, as verified by my English neighbours (neighbors) and teammates, Teri and Adrian.

The team's naming was left to them - neither I nor the other three Americans on the team familiar with the finer points of quiz night at the local pub. Teri then left it to Adrian, who promptly walked up to the scoreboard, a magic-markered grid on a giant pad of paper propped on an easel, and wrote, "Dickheads," in keeping with the English pub tradition of quiz night teams having inappropriate names.

The Dickheads would stick because also in attendance that night was a reporter from the *Gulf News*, Dubai's leading English-language newspaper with circulation in Qatar, Bahrain, Saudi Arabia, Kuwait, Oman, and Pakistan, as well as the UAE. There to report on expat life in Al Ain, in the *Gulf News* tabloid section the following week, September 17, 1991, was a feature on quiz night, complete with a full-color photo of the winning team… the "Richard Crowns," our team name deemed unfit for print. Disappointed but not surprised Dickheads didn't make the paper, even if we did, I was still delighted to know readers in Saudi Arabia were looking at a photo of Richard Crowns.

Usually, eight to twelve teams competed, answering questions from seven categories, including one audio, one category at a time. At the end of each round, answer sheets were swapped with a neighboring team for checking, like fifth-graders after taking a quiz, the quizmaster the teacher.

It was fun, but then there wasn't much to do in Al Ain in the days before satellite TV and the Internet. That's probably why quizmaster extraordinaire Colin, from Northern Ireland, ending each quiz night singing the Tom Jones classic "Delilah" with alcohol-induced feeling, was can't-miss entertainment.

The winning team received two bottles of champagne, each sealed with a real cork. Rarely drinking alcohol, especially champagne, all I got out of the prize were the corks, kept as toys for my cat, Tissa'a, cat toys, and sometimes cat food, hard to come by in Al Ain back in the day. Proper cat litter could be hard to find, too. If only there'd been a place where I could get some sand…

At the only other Western hotel, the Hilton, management realized they were losing out on what few Westerners there were in Al Ain, so the Hilton started a quiz night at their night spot, Paco's, or, as the Brits mispronounced it, "Pack-o's." With a Spanish name and matching motif, it was more lounge than pub, especially with the American woman who sang and played piano most nights, displaying far too much talent to be toiling in Al Ain.

Upping the ante, the Hilton awarded quiz night winners free dinners at Paco's or the hotel's swanky restaurant. They even gave away a bottle of champagne just for winning a category, popular with four-fifths of our team… and one cat. Much to the delight of the entire team, the InterCon then matched the Hilton's quiz night prize offerings.

As the wins kept coming, I dined in style at the hotels, for free, because even on those rare occasions when we lost, my quiz night meal was paid for, my teammates picking up the tab for being their all-time designated driver in a country with a zero tolerance drink/drive law. And if we won, not only were my fish and chips paid for, but so too was a sit-down dinner at a later date.

Most teams consisted of six players, which we were the first night, but only five after that - Teri and Adrian, Big John from Cleveland, and I, who all lived in the same villa complex, while Gus, from Chicago, lived but two roundabouts away, he replacing Anita and Tamara, they just not… Dickheads. The first year in Al Ain for all of us, all but Adrian taught at UAE University, he teaching at a private school and also tutoring a son of Shaikh Tahnoon bin Mohammed al Nahyan, ruler of the Abu Dhabi emirate's Eastern Region.

Most of the team, including me, worked afternoons and evenings, so we had to hustle to make quiz night on time. Even with the pedal to the metal, in the days before picture-taking radars when I could drive as fast as my car, nerve, and passengers would allow, more than a few times, the Dickheads didn't arrive until just before the quiz was about to begin. With the other quiz teams already seated, their hopes for victory elevated with our absence, they always greeted our last-minute arrival with a collective groan, "Augh! The Dickheads are here..." knowing we would likely be the free dinner winners.

With Lebanese folks knowing more than a thing or two about good food, our favorite was the Hilton's Lebanese Night in the hotel's main restaurant. And dinner there, in Arab tradition, was an all-night affair because when customers sat down at a table, it was theirs until closing, sometimes after midnight, sometimes well after midnight, even though the restaurant's posted closing time was 11 pm.

Most of the time, these dinners were Dickhead-only affairs, but nearing the end of our first school year, each team member had accumulated a pile of vouchers... with an expiration date. Wanting to use mine before they expired over my summer break, I invited seven colleagues from the Men's Campus at UAEU to an end-of-year dinner at Paco's.

The last time all of us would get together, the frivolity went on for hours. The pub's English manager and quizmaster, Brett, was pleased to have a table full of customers on what would've been an otherwise slow weekday night. Pleased, that is, until it came time to settle the bill, and I pulled out vouchers for eight free dinners, covering our $200-plus food tab.

"Dickhead!" exclaimed an exasperated Brett as he snatched the vouchers from my hand.

In contrast to Brett, our waitresses, Maria, a Filipina, and Maravic, a Sri Lankan, were all smiles. With extra cash in our pockets because dinner was on the Dickheads, we were especially generous with our tipping that night, knowing the ladies had not only taken good care of us but worked long hours, got little time off, lived in the hotel's employee housing, and were paid but a pittance.

"Hey, Brett! This might be the first night Maria and Maravic make more money than you!" …our back and forth all done in good fun. Probably. However, Brett and the hotel still had a good night, given the money we spent on drinks.

Owing to our success in the sleepy outpost, the Dickheads were what passed for celebrities in Al Ain, as everyone at the Hilton and InterCon Hotels knew our collective name. Including the waitresses, because when they brought the bill to our table, at the top, it always read, "Dickheads," even if it wasn't quiz night, even if we weren't all present.

For a quiz, if we were down a member or if someone was without a team, we accepted a straggler to be a Dickhead, if only for a night. I first realized we were a thing when one of my colleagues came up to me at work and asked, "Can I be a Dickhead?"

"Yes… yes, you can."

While our team name was Adrian's choice, we all had fun with it. "If we keep winning, everyone will want to be a Dickhead."

And we saw the potential for endorsements…

"Be a Dickhead, Drive a Honda"

"Buy Your Carpets From Mezon's. Dickhead's Do"
"Dickheads Shop Al Ahlia Prisunic"
"Paco's - Where Dickheads Hang Out"

After learning they started a quiz night, we also hung out at the Buraimi Hotel. Essentially a suburb of Al Ain, Buraimi was located just across the border in the Sultanate of Oman. The city's only Western-style hotel, the Buraimi was still nice, just not as fancy as Al Ain's Hilton or InterCon Hotels, Oman lacking the UAE's vast oil wealth.

The joke was, "1st Prize, a one-week stay at the Buraimi Hotel, 2nd prize, two weeks," but I always enjoyed my visits there, the border crossing adding a layer of non-existent intrigue to a night out. What I appreciated most was the hotel's friendly, home-grown staff because, unlike hotels in the UAE, Omanis, yes, Omanis staffed the front desk, waited on tables, cooked the food, cleaned the rooms, parked the cars, and greeted customers at the door. Real people with real jobs who seemed really happy when Westerners living in Al Ain crossed the border for some fun.

You might think the border crossing would've discouraged visits to Buraimi, and in a way, you'd be correct because, in the eight years I lived in Al Ain, I was never in Oman, officially anyway. But unofficially, I'd been there numerous times because all anyone had to do to cross the border was drive or walk over three speed bumps. It was just that easy... and exciting. Only if I drove further into Oman would I have to pass through a checkpoint with the proper paperwork.

Unfortunately, we missed the Buraimi Hotel's first few quiz nights, the other teams selfishly not sharing the news of the new competition, hoping the Dickheads wouldn't find out. But when we did, we were eager to compete, especially since the Buraimi Hotel, even though it was in another country, was closer to where we lived in Al Ain than the Hilton or the InterCon.

Even though the country had changed, the first time we walked into the lounge at the Buraimi Hotel for quiz night, the groan remained the same, "Augh! The Dickheads are here…" The results remained the same, too, for not only did we win our first night in Buraimi, but we would go undefeated in the Sultanate of Oman. Counting our seven victories in Buraimi, by the end of our three school years in Al Ain, the Dickheads won quiz night 57 times, a record that probably still stands.

But there would be no fourth year or 58th win for the Dickheads. After that third year, Big John and Gus moved back to the States, and toward the end of that third year, Teri and Adrian parted ways and would later divorce. Only myself and Teri, one of the few Westerners who outlasted me at UAE University, were all that remained of the Dickheads the following year.

We could've carried on, found replacements, and called our team the Dickheads, but it wouldn't be. How could it be? Because along with our collective knowledge, what made the Dickheads the Dickheads, despite Teri and Adrian's falling out, was the group's chemistry, camaraderie that couldn't be duplicated in a lab, a pub, or a club.

At the start of my fourth year in Al Ain, I went to a quiz night, playing on a team with some co-workers. Even though our team won, it just wasn't as much fun, or fun, because looking across the room at Teri, playing on another team, all I could think about was the good times that were… and were no more. Why I never went to another quiz night. I never missed it, though, content with the memories of the nearly three glorious years when I… when I was a Dickhead.

096

WE'RE LUCKY

I've never won a contest of luck. Not so much as a penny. I consider any money spent on games of chance to be a charitable donation. I figure if I ever won a lottery, the world would come to an end before I had the chance to cash in my ticket. As the hillbillies on *Hee-Haw* sang, "If it weren't for bad luck, I'd have no luck at all."

Grandma Curran would take me to bingo games in the Eau Claire area when I was a kid. You'd think that with an Irish Catholic grandmother named Mary Margaret at my side, I would've had the opportunity to shout "BINGO!" at least once. No such luck. Instead, I jinxed Grandma because she never got to yell "BINGO!" when I was around.

Maybe that's why we stopped spending Wednesday nights in church basements... or at least me. Nah, Grandma wouldn't leave me behind just to win at bingo. Maybe we stopped going because she figured, after so many losses, I'd learned my lesson - best not rely on luck to get ahead in this world, sonny boy.

But if The Strip in Las Vegas is any indication, I'm not the only unlucky person out there because it took a whole lot of "donations" to build all those glitzy casinos.

They sure didn't get built on the profits from their all-you-can-eat buffets, not off of me anyway. That's how I make my money because I can still pack away three days' worth of food in one sitting. I also make it a rule to never gamble more in a day than the cost of the casino's dinner buffet, my limit on what I'm willing to lose.

And I will lose because the math favors the casinos in every game, some more so than others. As I understand it, blackjack provides the best odds of winning, Keno the worst. That's fine with me because Keno looks like a bunch of older people in plaid sitting around staring at a screen, waiting for the numbers to change. I can see that at any Florida airport terminal.

While the house always has the odds advantage, compassionate sadists they are, casino operators are clever enough to give themselves only a slight edge. After all, how many gamblers would return to Vegas if the house won 90% of the time? Or 100%? Instead, the slight advantage the casinos enjoy, immensely, allows gamblers to win just enough to keep them coming back for more… losing.

But the long arm of the law of large numbers eventually catches up with gamblers. No matter how lucky they are, the math behind the casino's games will always prevail. The only way to win consistently is to cheat. That usually results in the cheater getting an escort to the front door from a thick-necked guy named Guido …at best. The only way to not lose is to walk away when you're ahead. Or, or, don't play at all.

With the math in their favor, the casinos have a business model that's impossible to beat. And I know the math. I used to teach it. As I explained to my Emirati students, "You know why gambling is haram in Islam? Because the casinos know math better than you do." I gave them the same reason for why Islam forbids charging interest on loans, substituting "banks" for "casinos."

While the UAE was a Muslim country, Ecuador is predominately Catholic, and they love their raffles. So, after we moved there, about every other month, a lovely local lady named Esperanza started appearing at our gate holding a stack of raffle tickets. Always priced at a dollar each, we keep a fiver lying around for when Esperanza comes around. I give her five dollars, and she gives me what always becomes five pieces of scrap paper for jotting down grocery lists.

The raffles are sponsored either by the barrio, the nearest town - San Pedro, a local church, or the monastery located just up the dead-end dirt (we aspire to gravel) road. What I like about the local raffles is that the grand prize is almost always a barnyard animal - a cow, horse, burro, or, in the last raffle I entered, a pig. That's how raffles roll in our barrio.

We never win... or do we? Because in contrast to not winning a pile of money, I find some comfort in knowing I didn't win a pig.

The five dollars is what it always is - a donation. But a fiver is not our only donation because the ink pen we use to fill out the raffle tickets always leaves with Esperanza as a much-appreciated gift. One of the best things about living where we do is that the locals appreciate the little things, even something as simple as a pen. In that regard, we're lucky.

097

BETWEEN DOGS AND FRANKS

<SPLAT!>

Even though I was traveling 60mph, the scene unfolded before me in slow motion.   Even so, there wasn't a thing I could do about it, boxed in on my right by the truck I'd just passed and on my left by a concrete median barrier.   A big ole raccoon had made it across two lanes of the freeway just south of Milwaukee. It did not make it across the third.   My only consolation was that it did not suffer.

After returning to Milwaukee after visits with friends and stadiums in Southern California, I attended classes for four days at UWM to reacquaint myself with my professors before I hit the road again to continue my research for my Master of Architecture thesis project.   This time, in Del's old Chrysler Cordoba with crushed velour upholstery, a sunroof, and an automatic transmission.

Filled with anticipation, I departed Milwaukee in the dark that Friday morning, hoping the early start would get me through Chicago before rush hour.   I just wish I'd left a little sooner or a little later because that <SPLAT!> would bother me the rest of my trip.

Poor raccoon.

Having cleared Chicago with little difficulty, I was well ahead of schedule to make the game at Tiger Stadium in Detroit that night. I was happy it wasn't a day game because the chilly morning had become an insufferably hot and humid afternoon.

"Sunroof!"

Not wanting to arrive in Detroit too early, I made an impromptu side trip to the University of Michigan campus in Ann Arbor. I hoped to get a look inside "The Big House," Michigan Stadium, home to the university's football team. And I did, after finding an unlocked gate and walking right in like I had every right to be there. And I did... but that was just my opinion.

The Big House was just that, the largest sports stadium in the United States and the second largest in the world, with a capacity of 107,601. Even though there was room for only 101,701 when I was there, standing alone in the stadium's vast seating bowl was unexpectedly... eerie.

Downtown Detroit was reputed to be "scary," but walking around "The Corner," Tiger Stadium's nickname owing to its location at the corner of Michigan and Trumbull Avenues, all I saw were die-hard baseball fans who loved their stadium as much as their team. Opened on April 20, 1912, the same day as Boston's Fenway Park, one of Tiger Stadium's most notable features was the upper seating deck, built directly above the lower deck instead of above and behind it.

The result was that spectators in the upper deck sat closer to the field of play than in any other major league ballpark. Those sitting in the lower deck, behind a column supporting the upper deck, were probably not as impressed. From my seat behind first base, in the upper deck, I felt as though I could reach out and touch the game. Seated in the upper deck in right field, I could've, as the front row overhung the field by ten feet, the result of a 1936 expansion that sought to maximize the number of seats given the limited space between the right field fence and Trumbull Avenue.

While the upper deck wrapped around the entire stadium, it didn't protect me from the wind. Neither did my jacket and travel vest - because I left them in the car, the weather still stifling when the stadium gates opened. But as they say in Wisconsin, "If you don't like the weather, wait 15 minutes."

They probably say the same thing in Michigan because, during the game, a massive cold front moved through Detroit. Sure, it felt great, for an inning or two, then not so much, as I was not yet ready for winter or dressed for it. But other than suffering from hypothermia, I enjoyed my first visit to Tiger Stadium.

Sadly, though, it would also be my last. Ten years later, the ballpark closed after the Tigers moved to a shiny new stadium. Ten years after that, despite desperate attempts by fans to save it, excavators, operated by men who I'm sure were only doing their job, demolished one of baseball's green cathedrals, Tiger Stadium.

Red Sox 9
Tigers 7
Attendance - 16,341

After the game, I didn't linger as I usually did. One, it was downtown Detroit, perhaps its scary reputation earned after dark. Two, I had an afternoon doubleheader to attend in Cleveland the following day. Three, I was freezing. And four, the Cordoba had a heater. But hot air wasn't the only thing blasting from the dashboard during the drive to Cleveland as I cranked the volume on the radio to help me stay awake.

And I know I was because somewhere around Toledo, I heard a news report that the high winds from the same cold front that blew through Detroit had blown a woman and her car - well, a Yugo - off the Mackinac Bridge connecting Michigan's Lower Peninsula with "da U-pee" (the Upper Peninsula). Speaking of eerie, when divers found the submerged Yugo containing her corpse 300 feet below the bridge deck under 150 feet of water, they reported the strong currents in the strait made it appear as though she was waving at them from inside the car...

When I got close enough to Cleveland that I knew I'd have no trouble making the midday start, I found a Marriott... parking lot. Better safe than sorry, I chose a spot under a light, visible from the hotel's entry, even though I figured no one would be hankering to break into an old Chrysler Cordoba. Using the front bucket seats as tent poles, I propped up a bed sheet between the front and back windows to give myself some privacy. "Blanket fort!"

Curled up in the back seat on the crushed velour upholstery, I managed to get some sleep before early risers woke me with the slamming of their car doors. Barely awake, I shuffled into the Marriott to find a public restroom. And I did, in addition to the hotel's complimentary breakfast buffet, where I helped myself. The sign said, "complimentary."

After breakfast, and after stuffing a banana or two into my jacket for later, I returned to the public restroom and took a "whore's bath," the slime from the previous day's sultry weather still clinging to my skin. Following a quick brush of the teeth, I was on my way to downtown Cleveland.

Just a stone's throw from Lake Erie, Municipal Stadium was known as "The Mistake On The Lake." The location wasn't a problem, as long as the wind wasn't blowing off the lake. But the wind was blowing off the lake with the passing of the cold front. Cloudy, windy, and downright cold, it was not a good day for baseball.

At the time, the stadium's capacity was a whopping (for baseball) 74,483. Given the lousy weather and that the Indians had long been eliminated from the playoffs probably had something to do with the many, many empty seats, over 65,000 of them. That wasn't eerie. That was depressing.

Even the rare two games for the price of one doubleheader was not enough to put bums in seats. With almost no one to slow me down, my research was done well before the first game was over. By the time the second game started, only a few hundred fans were left in the stands, as most had seen enough by the end of the first game.

With my work done and a long drive to Baltimore ahead of me, I should've left to get an early start. But in the upper deck, with so few spectators to compete with, I figured I'd never have a better chance for a personal first - catching a foul ball. Unfortunately, not one came my way. In addition, I'd never seen both halves of a major league doubleheader either. I had an opportunity to do so twice before, but the second game was rained out each time. So, wearing every shirt I'd packed for the trip and my jacket and vest, I stayed until the bitter (cold) end.

Angels 3
Indians 4

Angels 2
Indians 6
Attendance - 8,543

The scenery on that long drive to Baltimore, mainly across Pennsylvania, would've been lovely, except it rained most of the way and was dark all the way. I didn't have time to look around anyway because the Pennsylvania Turnpike was more of an obstacle course due to road construction. Even with the rain, the dark, and me more than a little tired, I somehow managed to avoid every orange barrel.

Poor raccoon.

But the biggest obstacle came when I tried to exit the Pennsylvania Turnpike late that Saturday night because my research on the cost of driving the tollway proved flawed. The toll taker wanted twice what I expected. Seconds later, I also learned they did not accept credit cards.

Even though it was only day two of my trip, and despite my complimentary breakfast buffet at the Marriott, I was low on cash. So low that there was not enough in my wallet to pay the man. Reduced to scrounging the car seats and floor for loose change, I made up the difference, eventually, with a quarter to spare. If you were behind me in line, I apologize.

With only a bit more fuel than cash, I had to find a service station, open late, that accepted credit cards, which I did just before crossing into Maryland. Just in time because when I pulled alongside the pump, the Cordoba shuddered out of gas. I rarely think about my credit card being denied… but I did that night.

After entering Maryland and not far from Jay's, with that last quarter, I called and told him where I was so he could come to meet me. I then followed him home, my first visit to his newish house. It was after midnight when I finally arrived at Jay and Jean's house south of Baltimore, near the BWI airport. It was even later by the time I got set up on their sofa. With three young children in the house, Jayme, A.J., and Joey, I knew I'd be up early, even on a Sunday.

And I was.

While I would've preferred to kick back and relax that day, there'd be no rest for the weary because that afternoon, we had tickets for the Orioles' last home game of the season, my last chance to see Memorial Stadium, "The Old Gray Lady of 33rd Street." Or, as it was known for Colts football games, "The World's Largest Outdoor Insane Asylum." While my Uncle Mike confirmed the nickname appropriate for football several years before my visit, for baseball, the crowd wasn't quite so cuckoo.

After the miserable weather in Detroit and Cleveland, I enjoyed the warm, sunny day almost as much as the game. And with a near-capacity crowd, I didn't see many empty seats after seeing 200,000 during my three previous stadium visits. Although it was a great day for baseball, Orioles fans went home disappointed as the hated Yankees prevailed.

I was used to the hometown team losing as I'd seen the Brewers play twelve times at County Stadium in Milwaukee, and twelve times they lost. I wouldn't get to another Brewers home game until the following July. However, I bought tickets for that game a month in advance, hoping to see them lose and Texas Rangers pitcher Nolan Ryan win, which he did for his 300th career victory, securing his place in baseball's Hall of Fame.

I've only been to one Brewer home game since, at the new stadium, but the venue change made no difference. Neither did taking Sue to her first big league baseball game, as I saw the Brewers lose in Milwaukee for the fourteenth time in fourteen games.

Yankees 2
Orioles 0
Attendance - 51,173

I visited with Jay and his family until Thursday. Did some laundry. Restocked my supply of traveling munchies. Ate something other than stadium food. Showered. Slept. I also traded some credit card purchases on Jay's behalf for cash, enough to get me back to Milwaukee - I then with a better idea of how much I'd need.

Naturally curious about the purpose of my travels, Jayme, who'd just turned ten, had questions. And, as children that age often do, she got right to it.

"Where'd you come from, Unka John?"

"Cleveland."

"Where are you going next?"

"Boston."

"Then where?"

"New York, Buffalo, Toronto, Chicago…"

"Don't your teachers care you're skipping school?"

"No."

"DAAAAD! Can I…"

"NO!"

098

HELLO… GOODBYE

"Mister John, you sure can pick'em," I thought to myself as I was deciding which airport, Abu Dhabi or Dubai, I preferred to fly out of after being fired and then deported. But as far as I know, her father - both the boss and the dean where I worked - never found out about us, nor did anyone who could've sent me packing… or worse. Even her brother, a colleague and friend, didn't learn of his sister's and my relationship until many months later, and then only after she clued him in.

Friends before I met his sister, I hoped he knew I was uncomfortable not telling him the whole truth in our conversations after I did. When it came to social norms in the United Arab Emirates, and pretty much anywhere within a thousand miles, one of the things that never sat right with me was that they made liars out of almost everyone. One Emirati woman I remain friends with, who, when talking about keeping her boyfriend a secret, once told me, "I hate this. I'm 33 years old, and I still have to lie to my parents."

Even though I had to engage in deception to maintain our privacy, I was not about to walk away, even after learning who her father was and the risks entailed. She never brought up the subject, and I never asked. Presumably, she'd known all along who her father was, so there was no need for me to ask if we were an issue. Surely, she'd let me know if our relationship ever became one.

One night, she did, when I was never so cold… in Al Ain anyway.

During the first of my eight years there, smoke from the oil well fires in Kuwait blotted out the northwest sky during the day. Not only did that smoke wreak havoc with Iran's pistachio crop (for that alone, Saddam deserved to hang), but the reduced sunshine resulted in unusually "cold" temperatures in Al Ain, one of the hotter places on Earth. So, in the middle of what passed for winter, I was shivering, after dark, in a park, sitting on a bench. She was also shivering, so gentleman that I was, I offered her my windbreaker. Which she happily accepted, I then even colder.

Even so, there was no place I'd rather be than with her, especially on Valentine's Day. Because on that day, you're happy to share your connection with another… or you're alone. More years than not, I was the latter, with the mindset, "This day can't end soon enough." But I would spend that Valentine's Day with the woman of my dreams, one I'd been secretly seeing since we met in a library four months before.

On that bench, in a far corner of the park, we exchanged gifts, and then, somehow, we ended up holding hands, if ever so briefly, the first and only time we ever touched. I don't know if she'd ever held hands with a man before, as it seemed a new experience for her and one that meant something. For me, too, if only because the hand I held was hers.

"John… I have something to tell you."
"Me too, but ladies first."

The subject had come up a time or two before - the where of her near future. Her options were to study for a postgraduate degree in Cairo, go to London to do the same, or work in the United Arab Emirates for another year. I, of course, was hoping for the latter but knew it was the least likely choice for her to make.

And it was, as she explained, as delicately as she could, that she'd decided to continue her studies in Cairo. If she'd gone to London, at least I could've visited her during holidays, in a Western country where our togetherness, in public, wouldn't have been an issue. It was about not to matter anyway…

"John… I don't think we should see each other anymore. We'd just be delaying the inevitable."

"…"

I wasn't bleeding. My bones weren't broken. There were no cuts, scrapes, or bruises. I would've passed a physical with flying colors. Yet, all I could feel was pain. It was maybe the only time I ever completely lost it. I couldn't see. I couldn't hear. I couldn't even feel how cold I was. And after what she said, there wasn't much point in what I had to say.

Taking me from the highest high to the lowest low, no words ever hurt so much, as there was no one I wanted to be with more than her. Even though we'd known each other for only four months, I felt like I'd known her always. But now, a disembodied voice inside my head was telling me, "John… wake up… dream's over… time to return to reality."

She Muslim, me not, from the start, ours was an improbable relationship. While she knew that, I… was… ignorant… blissfully ignorant. Yes, I was aware such relationships were contrary to the local norms and the reasons why - why we had to keep our relationship a secret. Living in the UAE for only a few months, though, there was still so much I didn't understand. Fully understand.

Even knowing what little I knew, I was the think-big boy I'd always been, believing anything I could dream was possible - that there was always a way. If I'd thought we had no future, I could've avoided her, the pain of a broken heart, and four of the best months of my life. That's why I never regretted my decision to become involved with her, and then, after discovering who her father was, remain involved with her.

Yet it was not her father or even her brother that ended our relationship, but "rules," silly, human rules, the kind I never liked, the "because it's a rule" rules. With more experience living in the UAE, I would grudgingly accept that we never had a chance because her family and culture wouldn't allow it, even if her religion would. Even so, I would experience one more such broken heart before finally learning my lesson.

So, given what she knew far better than I, just as our telephone conversations often had to end not because we wanted them to but because they had to, so too did our relationship. There is an ever-shrinking part of me still bitter that we never had a chance; the game rigged against me, against us. However, that feeling has helped me appreciate those who live a lifetime facing unnecessarily difficult odds for no other reason than they are who they are. While I sometimes wonder what might've been, I'm grateful for what was - that our paths were one, long enough for us to enjoy each other's company until it was time to go our separate ways.

A few months later, she did indeed return to Egypt. I'd hoped for a last-minute reprieve, that somehow, somehow… but it was not to be. Her last day in the UAE was almost as sad for me as that Valentine's Day night in the park. She was leaving, and I could only wish her well, in a second-floor hallway of my office building, one of the least romantic places in the world, where we said our goodbyes.

I visited Egypt the following summer on holiday with Ma in tow. We arranged to meet her in Cairo, where she gave us a day tour of her hometown, highlighted by an extended stop at the historic Khan el-Khalili bazaar. I so wished I could've returned the favor, not that my hometown could compare with one featuring the Pyramids, the Sphinx, or the treasures of King Tut, but still…

While I was overjoyed to see her again and spend some precious time with her, I was well aware that every minute together brought me closer to the last I ever would. Eventually, those minutes were down to a handful. Knowing the end was near, the ride down the elevator with her at the Ramses Hilton Hotel was simultaneously the longest and shortest of my life. If ever there was a time to get stuck in an elevator…

Unless they're on their deathbed, usually, you never know the last time you see someone will be the last, but this time, this time, I knew. On the street outside the hotel, amid the cacophony of traffic around the east end of the 6th of October Bridge, a major Nile River crossing, the Pyramids and the Sphinx less than six miles away, the treasures of King Tut on display in the museum across the street, we said our goodbyes… for the final time.

Desperate for just one more minute with her, I'd not get it as there was no delay in bagging a taxi, not when a pretty girl was doing the hailing. She climbed in the back seat, then closed the door, the taxi pulling away, with only the shadowy silhouette of her head visible in the back window. It all happened so fast… in painfully slow motion…

Tears streamed down my face as her taxi motored up the on-ramp to the bridge. Even though I was standing in a city of over 15 million people, I never felt so alone after the car carrying the person I most wanted by my side... faded from view. That the last time I saw her, I recalled the first - when the sight of her left me so lost for words I couldn't manage even a "Hello," and now... now I couldn't bear to hear, much less say "Goodbye."

099

A TRIANGLE WITH 3 RIGHT ANGLES

"Penguins live on the equator."

"No, they don't."

"Yes, they do."

My fourth grade teacher, Mrs. Sizer, didn't believe me. Challenged in front of the class, I consulted the encyclopedia, just steps away, the Internet and Google still several years away. Sure enough, according to the World Book, there were indeed penguins living on the equator in Ecuador's Galapagos Islands. Teachers didn't know everything, but then little did I know I'd be living in Ecuador 35 years later.

Two years later, in sixth grade, my desk and I sat in a back row corner, a map of the world to our immediate right. No doubt it was one reason why my eyes were seldom front, and World Geography has long been a favorite *Jeopardy* category. I've always liked maps, which is why Google Earth is one of my favorite apps.

One day, my teacher, Mrs. Biever, made her way to my back corner to have a look at the world map, one of those giant flip maps mounted on a tripod. Sensing she was having trouble, I asked, "What are you looking for, Mrs. Biever?"

"Uruguay."

Looking in Eastern Europe, no wonder she was having trouble. So I reached over and pointed to the small splotch of yellow sandwiched between Brazil and Argentina in South America.

"Uruguay."

"You know your geography, Mr. Curran," as she tapped me on the head with her rolled-up papers.

Teachers didn't know everything, but students sometimes thought they did, believing whatever they were taught to be true, even if the teacher got it wrong. Wish that I could, but I don't remember what grade it was when I was taught, "Don't end a sentence with a preposition." Over the years, "grammar Nazis" went off on me for doing just that. Yet many respected linguists have no problem with sentences ending with "with."

But I still hear, "It's wrong," because someone once told these language fascists, "It's wrong," and probably never explained why because there is no real reason why. So when I ask, "Why?" their only answers are, "That's what I was taught," or worse, "It's a rule."

"Yeah, well, ending a sentence with a preposition is not something I have a problem with."

And like me, you were probably taught in school that a triangle can only have one right angle because the sum of the interior angles must add up to 180 degrees. With two right angles, each 90 degrees, the third angle must be 0 degrees, and an angle of 0 degrees is no angle, so no triangle. It's a rule even the most geometrically challenged almost always remember.

The students in the art class at Waupaca High School, where I was invited to speak while home on winter break from my studies at the University of Wisconsin-Milwaukee, certainly remembered. For what was a class of high school seniors, I was meant to talk about my years of university experience, answer questions, offer advice, etc., for those about to join me in acquiring a higher education and student loan debt.

Looking around the room, I noticed most couldn't have cared less that I was sacrificing my precious time off for their benefit. Having been a teenager for a year or two, I'm going to go ahead and state that most thought they knew all there was to know, and in my twenties, to them, I was already an old person. How could I possibly know anything relevant? Or be trusted?

Starting a trend that would continue when I became a teacher, I didn't stick to the script after sensing the students needed a different kind of lesson than the one planned. So to get their attention and to show them that maybe they didn't know everything, I began with a request.

"Show me a triangle with three right angles."

The unexpected challenge got their attention, as they knew a triangle with three right angles was impossible and were eager to point that out to me. So eager, not one student even considered the question before hitting me with their daggers of resistance...

"Impossible!"

"No way!"

"Can't do it!"

"A triangle can only have one right angle!"

To which I responded, "The answer is right in front of you. You see it every day, an example of a triangle with three right angles."

"Where?"

"I don't see one!"

"It's right in front of you," I stated.

"Impossible!"

"No way!"

"Can't do it!"

"A triangle can only have one right angle!"

And there was an example right in front of them, for on a shelf behind me was a world globe. I hoped there'd be one student who knew the answer, but none did. As it turned out, the lesson was probably better because no one did. Having given up on finding the elusive answer right in front of them, most grabbed their sketchpads and attempted to draw a triangle with three right angles. They were, after all, art students.

One showed me a drawing of three triangles, each with one right angle, hoping it was the answer. It was not.

Another drew an equilateral triangle and a forced box in each corner, the kind used to denote an angle of 90 degrees, hoping that would make it so. It did not.

Another showed me a drawing of a right triangle with two more right triangles drawn inside the first, hoping they had the correct answer. Clever, but no.

After a furious five or so minutes of scribbling, most were never more certain there was no such thing as a triangle with three right angles.

"Impossible!"

"No way!"

"Can't do it!"

"A triangle can only have one right angle!"

They were correct, in Euclidean (standard high school geometry), where a triangle has three sides and three interior angles measuring 180 degrees, so a triangle with three right angles totaling 270 degrees is impossible. However, a triangle with three right angles is possible in non-Euclidean or spherical geometry. Spherical, like the world globe behind me.

Plucking it from the shelf, I demonstrated that if I started at the North Pole and went south along 0 degrees longitude until I reached the equator, west along the equator for 90 degrees, and north along the 90-degree longitude line to the North Pole, I outlined a triangle with three right angles.

Amazed by my demonstration, they all got down on the floor in the prone position, then raised their arms, hailing me for having released them from a lifetime of triangular ignorance, for showing them that what was impossible was not and that their geometry teacher, while not wrong, was not correct either. With open arms and open minds, they accepted this new truth, vowing to spend the remainder of their lives setting the one right-angle triangle record straight.

Yeah… that didn't happen.

Instead, I got a room full of highly agitated high school students even more galvanized in their belief that a triangle with three right angles was…

"Impossible!"

"No way!"

"Can't do it!"

"A triangle can only have one right angle!"

"Three sides… three right angles," I said as I ran my finger along the globe, outlining a triangle with three sides and three right angles.

"You can't do that!"

"That's not a triangle!"

"But!..."

That no one gave an acceptable answer was not what disappointed me. What did was that when shown one, they protested, many passionately, clinging to their rule like my mother to the handrail on Colorado's Royal Gorge Bridge a thousand feet above the Arkansas River.

Most probably didn't like math, nor the teacher who taught them triangles could only have one right angle, but they accepted what they were told anyway. After they were told, their minds closed - to other possibilities, contexts, and answers. So years later, they refused to relinquish their known known when shown what they'd been taught was only conditionally true.

After they'd calmed down, after the lynch mob in the back put away their rope, I chided them, "This is an art class. It's the one class where there should be no rules. Anything you can imagine should be possible. Just because a teacher once told you something doesn't make it so. A triangle can't have more than one right angle in a two-dimensional world, but in a three-dimensional world, where you live, it can."

Knowing I would get no further with the class on the triangle with three right angles, I used my demonstration to bring the conversation around to what, I think, I was supposed to talk about.

"A university is a place to question everything." I thought kindergarten was, probably why I was sent to the principal's office more in my first year of school than all the rest combined.

There may have been one, maybe two students who got it, my point, if not a solution for a triangle with three right angles. However, being teenagers, they would've been too cool for school to admit that - peer pressure doing more to dumb down a classroom than even the worst teacher. What the students learned that day, if anything, I would never know.

Although I wouldn't realize it until later, I learned that a high school art class wasn't a place to go off script, challenge students, or inspire them to question authority and the status quo because I was never invited back. At least I wasn't sent to the principal's office.

That seems like a good line to end this story with.

100

MAY DAY, 1994

"Why did you retire and move to Ecuador when you were just 44?" It's a question I've been asked many times since I did just that in July 2007. Because there were so many factors behind my decision, I've probably never given the same answer twice. But there's one I've never given, a memory I've never voiced, only written. This one…

I don't remember everything I did on May Day, 1994, but I know I watched an auto race, the Formula 1 San Marino Gran Prix. Back then, Ayrton Senna was regarded as the best F1 driver of the time and possibly of all time. Many still regard him as the best, and he remains a national hero in his home country of Brazil.

While his name is as unrecognizable to many Americans as Sachin Tendulkar's, the auto-racing world knows his name well because Ayrton Senna had that certain something only a few stars have beyond the skill required to be a champion. That something put bums in seats, including mine, in front of my TV that day. Thanks to the government of the United Arab Emirates making it legal for me to install a satellite dish on the roof of my villa in Al Ain, I could watch the race on Star TV, headquartered in Hong Kong.

Even before I moved overseas, I was a fan of Formula 1, rightly regarded as the pinnacle of auto racing. Many of the advances in modern production vehicles directly result from F1 racing. That technology and the skill required to push it to the limit, along with the "exotic" race locations and the international field of competitors, attracted me to the motorsport.

If you've never been to the spectacle that is a Formula 1 race, go, even if you're not a fan of racing, you'll be glad you did. Bring earplugs because engines on F1 cars can hit 20,000rpm, while your neighbor's noisy car probably red lines at 5000. I know if I won the lottery, I'd spend a year going to every race, if nothing else, just to travel... and do some international people-watching, as I did at the only Formula 1 race I've ever attended, the 1989 British Gran Prix at the Silverstone Circuit in England.

Ayrton Senna spun out of the lead at Silverstone that day, allowing his teammate, Frenchman Alain Prost, to beat home-crowd favorite Nigel Mansell across the finish line. On May Day, 1994, as I watched the San Marino Gran Prix in Imola, Italy, on Star TV, Ayrton Senna was also in the lead. But on lap 7, due to a mechanical failure, Senna's car spun off at the Tamburello curve at 190mph, crashing into a concrete barrier at 135mph.

An overhead TV camera zoomed in on what was left of his race car. As the camera brought viewers in for a closer look, I expected Senna to remove the steering wheel and hoist himself out of the wreckage. Instead, he just sat there. Then his head leaned a bit to the left and then slumped back.

A three-time Formula 1 world champion, Ayrton Senna had it all and then some - fame, fortune, and everything else that comes with being a star in an international sport - including the adoration of millions of fans in Brazil and millions more around the world. But just like that, Ayrton Senna's life was over. He was just 34 years old.

The crash resulted in numerous safety improvements in Formula 1, which kept Senna's name the last on the list of F1 driver racing fatalities for 20 years. Some of those safety enhancements are now a part of your car. If you've been in an auto accident since 1994, maybe you're alive to read this because of Senna's crash and the efforts of those who sought to make sure an accident like his never happened again.

Good things can come from bad. While car and racetrack designers learned some valuable lessons from that day in May, bums in seats, including mine, got a vivid reminder of just how quickly everything we have can be lost, even if we're not Formula 1 drivers. It's a reminder I get every May Day simply because I remember watching that race...

Experience has shown me that life consists of mostly forgettable days sprinkled with a few memorable ones - some good, some bad. While the good ones inspire me to make more such memories, the bad ones can serve a purpose, too. Witnessing Senna's fatal crash got me thinking. About not taking what I had for granted, to live life on my terms sooner rather than later after realizing at 31 that my last curve could be just around the corner.

So when I have a good day, sometimes I think of Ayrton Senna's fatal crash, knowing part of the reason why I'm enjoying my life is the lesson I learned that day in May. Remembering that crash also reminded me to drive far more carefully than I had been so I wouldn't have an accident and become the reason someone else's day was one they'd like to forget.

101

THE AWFUL TOWER

In July 2006, Sue and I traveled to Ecuador to check out a property because we had a good idea of what it had and didn't know what it didn't. Lee's brochure describing the property was good, but there's no substitute for doing boots-on-the-ground due diligence. Sure, I bought my first car in a foreign country without seeing it first, but I wasn't about to buy a house in a foreign country that way. Not for another decade, anyway...

While Sue and I discovered there was more good stuff than we thought - like two bamboo groves and all kinds of fruit trees - we also learned the property had no street address, home mail delivery (probably related to the no street address thing), municipal water, street lights, garbage pick-up, landline telephone service, cable TV, enclosed kitchen, bathroom accessible without going outside, paved road access, or gravel road access. Oh, and no bidet.

Sue and I bought the property anyway - none of the above a deal breaker for either of us. Before you think all the good stuff swayed us into buying a problem property, it didn't. We'd already passed on several otherwise good properties because they didn't meet all our criteria, knowing if we settled for less, that's exactly what we'd get.

Instead, as always, we stuck to our criteria list, and this property ticked every box that mattered to us:

Rural mountain setting
Good weather
Healthy environment
Clean water
Good food
A bit of land
Enough house to live in while renovating
English or Spanish-speaking people
$75,000 or less sale price

Oh, and one more thing - Internet service. The property, a couple-two-three miles outside Vilcabamba, didn't have Internet, but we were surprised and then pleased to learn that service was available. Sometimes, though, I wonder if we would've purchased the then acre-and-a-half of dream-come-true if we'd known just how awful that service would be.

We'd find out a year later, after moving from the United Arab Emirates, where Etisalat, our former ISP, provided cheap, reliable, albeit censored access. Backing that service were seven, seven undersea cables providing bandwidth and redundancy, proving their worth after fishing trawlers severed four of them over two weeks.

When we moved to Ecuador, the country had only one undersea cable providing Internet access, but at least the government didn't censor our service. The tradeoff was a huge drop in speed and reliability - back to the good old days of dial-up - as we paid our ISP the princely sum of $50 per month for 384K service. 384K. When it worked.

We had no one to blame but ourselves, purchasing the property without vetting the service. To feel better about that, I reminded myself that having any Internet off a dead-end dirt road on the side of a mountain in a remote part of Ecuador bordered on the miraculous. I also reminded myself that I moved to the UAE, then lived there for years without the Internet, and survived to write about it.

Points I struggled to remember when service was slow, slower than 384K, as it often was, or just down, sometimes because our ISP's transmitter tower was down... on the ground.

If you're envisioning one of the now ubiquitous towers that have sprouted across the connected world since smartphones and tablets became a thing, uh... no. Our ISP's tower, propped against an outbuilding on a property across the valley from ours, was a bamboo pole. When the wind blew with fury, which it can do during the dry season, the bamboo pole blew too... over.

When our Internet went out on a windy day, it was the first thing we'd check because other than a power failure, "tower down" was the easiest diagnosis - the zoom lens on my camera enough to verify the tower's status. If it wasn't down, then we performed diagnostics to assess the problem. Knowing a thing or two about computers - Sue a former computer technician, and I, a former computer teacher - we could.

The first time our Internet went down because the tower went down, Sue called our ISP to inform them. As is the modus operandi of seemingly all telecom providers, even a pop (no mom) operation in Vilcabamba, the man in charge told Sue there was no problem, his computer indicating the system was working fine, so the problem must be on our end.

"We can see your tower from our house. The wind blew it over."

"Oh."

Half an hour or so later, the zoom lens on my camera was enough to watch him and his crew of two put the bamboo pole back into place, Internet restored.

Still, ours was but a 384K connection. That was on a good day, when there wasn't some other problem, and there were problems. For one, our ISP got his service via radio transmitters through the mountains between Vilcabamba and Loja, where landslides, high winds, heavy rain, passing clouds, or burros with itchy bums could disrupt service. Frustrating was not the word, especially since the Internet was our only connection to the outside world.

Frustrating was not the word for it either after I lost hundreds of dollars when a days-long outage prevented me from resetting a savings account to not roll over for a year, and the foreign currency, as I knew it would, dropped significantly in value versus the U.S. dollar.

"ARGH!"

At the time, there was only one ISP in Vilcabamba, so my only other viable option was to make a trip to Loja and try resetting that savings account at an Internet cafe. Logging on to my bank at some dodgy hole-in-the-wall establishment sounded even riskier than rolling over an account poised to lose value. Ah well. As my best friend Dan often reminds me, "It's only money."

A few years later, Internet service in Ecuador improved with the addition of a second undersea cable. Originating in Miami and passing through Panama, it increased bandwidth while providing much-needed redundancy. We still paid $50 per month, but our bandwidth eventually increased from 384K to 6MB. Reliability improved as well, but the Internet still went out too frequently, and our bandwidth would often drop below 384K, sometimes for days.

When it did, Sue contacted our ISP. Even if she could tell the person answering the phone what the problem was - by then, her Spanish was at least as good as mine - more often than not, she was told the system was working fine, so the problem must be on our end. Some things never change. Some did, though, as our ISP lost its monopoly in the Vilcabamba area after other providers moved in following the influx of expats.

Customers then rotated their loyalties based on which ISP was having fewer problems because they all did and responded in a similar defensive fashion when told so. We, too, had switched providers after learning our ISP continued charging us $50 per month when new customers were getting more bandwidth for the same or lower price despite our often providing spot-on and free troubleshooting assistance.

The ISPs also upgraded their equipment - we then connected to a transmitter mounted on a proper steel tower next to another steel tower that replaced the bamboo one. Located further down the valley, my zoom lens was no longer enough to check its status... unless I was up on the roof of our house for a change in perspective, to take photos, prune trees, spy on the neighbors, or check on our Internet antenna, mounted on a steel pole attached to the house.

Our ISP's steel tower never blew over in the wind, although lightning struck it once, damaging equipment and severely degrading service for a few weeks. Another worry was that the tower was next to a sugar cane mill that caught fire a few times. We didn't worry so much about the tower catching fire, but the equipment mounted on it melting and delivery of replacement parts, as we experienced following the lightning strike, weeks away.

Our main problem, though, was maintaining a clear line of sight between the ISP's transmitter and our receiver when I could do what I could not in Wisconsin - watch trees grow. Beating back the greenery was a struggle, one that required me to stand on our sloped back porch roof, reach up with a rake in hand to snag a branch, then pull it down and trim it with my machete.

Then, there were the trees encroaching on that clear line of sight I couldn't reach on the neighboring property, which would've forced us to install a longer pole for our antenna. Or buy the lot next door, then trim the trees, as I'm not about to cut down one just to get Internet. As a neighbor up the road did, paying a guy to cut several huilco trees to restore her clear line of sight. An aggressive solution, for a renter, especially since the trees, sacred to the Incas (Vilcabamba, roughly translated as "Huilco Valley"), are supposedly protected by local law.

So when there was talk of ISPs installing fiber optic cable, Sue and I were hopeful. But not optimistic, given Vilcabamba had cable TV before our first journey here, but in the interim 14 years, that service had never extended beyond the town limits. Then there was my conversation with surveyors in September 2007, just two months after we moved here. Wondering what they were doing, painting numbers on our brick wall fronting the road, they explained the municipality would be installing streetlights, a project they said would be completed by year's end.

We didn't care whether we got streetlights or not, as we lived in a rural area, but silly me, I should've asked, "Which year?" as the painted numbers were still on our wall when the streetlights were finally installed... almost 17 years later.

"Fiber optic cable is coming by the end of the year? Which year?" As it turned out, that year. A few months later, there was a crew on the road stringing cable between utility poles for what they told Sue was soon to be available Internet service. Soon came soon enough, as shortly after that, workers connected us to the Internet via fiber optic cable. We were the first on our dead-end dirt (we aspired to gravel) road to have the service installed.

Connecting to the nearest junction box required the stringing of 292 additional meters of the small, strong, and lightweight cable. With the regular installation price, $40, based on no more than 100 meters, we paid a "whopping" $88 extra. Watching Christian and Juan string the cable, I wondered how much it would've cost us in the States or Canada.

With the help of a bamboo pole to get it up and over the greenery, Christian and Juan strung the cable from the nearest utility pole, in a neighbor's property, to the same mast where our power line came in. I then threaded the cable into a plastic tube buried in our topiary bougainvillea (as was done for the power line) and then through a hole I drilled in our home's foot-and-a-half-thick rammed earth walls. Inside, Christian and Juan then made the final connection to a Wi-Fi router, Huawei brand, so no doubt Chinese intelligence agents then started spying on us.

As a result of the infrastructure upgrade, our connection improved from 6MB to 10MB, but the price remained the same, $30 per month, with no limit on data. A year or so later, we had 50MB service for the same price, and the reliability proved outstanding. If we'd wanted, we didn't, we could've gotten cable TV and a landline telephone via the same connection. Best of all, we no longer had to worry about maintaining a clear line of sight to a transmitter tower or service degrading or dropping when the wind blew, it rained, the mill burned, again, or because some burro had an itchy bum.

After Christian and Juan left, I had a moment, the kind I've only experienced as an expat - the satisfaction of getting something done in a foreign country, and in a foreign language. The same feeling I got each year after registering my car in less than 30 minutes at the notorious Al Ain Traffic Police - as rewarding as any of the many experiences I've had as an expat.

That and almost 13 years after we received our Internet service via a radio transmitter mounted on a bamboo pole, it arrived via fiber optic cable. Amazed I had such service on the side of a mountain in a remote part of Ecuador when family and friends in the States did not, I wondered aloud, after double-checking my connection speed, "What's next? Gravel?"

102

C'MON, JOHNNY, FINISH'ER UP

"You got AIDS?" That was the first thing Dan said to me my first summer back in Wisconsin after teaching in the United Arab Emirates.

Dan always hated summers, his kitchen at the Waupaca Woods Restaurant was always too hot, even though he rarely wore more than a tank top, shorts, an apron, probably some shoes, maybe socks, and, hopefully, underwear. Because you never know when the restaurant inspector would drop by, unannounced, and from what Dan told me, he checked everything. Everything.

Meanwhile, I'd just returned from Al Ain, where 90 degrees was a cool night in summer, so wearing a jacket, I purposely planted myself in front of his grill, warming my hands…

"Bit chilly in here."

Dan gave me a look that said what he did not, but friends we were, I understood. Because Dan and I could carry on a conversation without saying anything, much to the chagrin of those around us who knew we were talking but not so they could hear. Just a series of looks and gestures - our version of sign language - was all we needed sometimes, knowing each other so well for so long. Why Dan noticed I'd lost weight, even though I was wearing a jacket.

His question was fitting, even if my clothes weren't, especially since I'd heard many in the UAE refer to AIDS as "thin man disease." I did not have AIDS, but that first year in the UAE, I didn't have a stove either, partly contributing to my weight loss. And working nights, I often came home and ate whatever was easy to make on my two-burner hotplate - like pasta, elevating it only with the addition of salt, pepper, and butter... after boiling it in water, of course.

While I could afford to, I wasn't eating as well as I did during my six years at the University of Wisconsin-Milwaukee. That's not saying much. With only the 5-lunch plan from the university cafeteria, because that's all I could afford, I smuggled out as much all-you-can-eat food as I could in the oversized pockets of my big blue winter coat, nothing in my meal plan saying when I had to eat that food. Fortunately, winters in Wisconsin were longer back then because wearing that coat on warm days looked mighty suspicious to overly observant cafeteria workers.

With no cafeteria lunches on Saturdays and Sundays, I made do with a West Bend 6-Cup Hotpot, used to prepare Kraft Macaroni & Cheese, SpaghettiOs, or Campbell's Soup to go with whatever I'd managed to smuggle out of the cafeteria Monday through Friday. And no matter the day of the week, if I was hungry, which I often was, I got out my West Bend 4-quart popcorn popper. OK, I never had to get it out because I never put it away, as almost every night, and sometimes twice on Sundays, during football season, I used it to pop corn. In case you were wondering, yellow, not white, topped with all-you-can-eat butter patties and salt courtesy of the dorm cafeteria.

For my second year in Al Ain, I bought a proper stove, or "cooker," as they were called in the UAE, with four burners to make what I made the previous year with only two. And I finally had an oven, perfect for warming up leftover pizza from Pizza Hut. While my intentions were good, I didn't use my new cooker more than I had the hotplate.

That changed after I hired Jaya (Jeye-uh), a spunky Sri Lankan, to clean my villa once a week. Even though she was a "lowly" housemaid and five-foot-nothing, she had no trouble speaking her mind, even to her part-time employer. So it wasn't long before Jaya felt comfortable enough to scold me, with my nearly empty refrigerator, for not eating like I should and could.

"You rich man. Eat like poor man."

Jaya had a point. I could afford to eat better. More importantly, I couldn't afford not to, my body not as young as it used to be. So, with Jaya's help, I started eating as I should because not only could she clean my villa within an inch of a hospital operating room, but she was also a darn good cook. And a good teacher, too, as I learned more about preparing food that year than I ever imagined I would.

Armed with family favorite recipes I collected from Ma my first summer back in Wisconsin, at Jaya's insistence, I started baking - bread, cookies, cakes, pies - desserts of all kinds. She even learned a thing or two about baking, including how to make something she'd never seen before, much less eaten, pumpkin pie, or as she referred to it, "baby poop pie." To get her to take that first bite took some coaxing. The second did not, especially after I added a dollop of whipped cream as a reward for taking the first.

With my university eating habits finally behind me, not only did I feel better, I started gaining weight.

So when I dropped by Dan's kitchen my second summer back, his first remark was not about my weight but my grooming habits. Mostly because I hated shaving, especially in a locale that was so hot and dry, I'd spent my second year in Al Ain perfecting the permanent scruff look.

"Johnny, try standing a little closer to the razor tomorrow morning."

And he still gave me that look after I once again purposely planted myself in front of his grill, wearing my jacket, warming my hands, in July.

"Bit chilly in here."

Dan did his best to ensure I never left his kitchen hungry, though. He always prepared a plate for me, or if an order got messed up, he'd give it to me to eat. In return, I did my best to stay out of the way - if you can't stand and eat, get out of the kitchen.

Even when I'd forgo an out-of-the-way kitchen corner to dine with the rest of his customers, I still got plenty of good food to eat, especially when I stopped by for breakfast before catching my first flight back to the UAE. With a long journey ahead, I always ordered the rib eye steak and eggs breakfast, made even more filling when Dan would send out the waitress with a double order and a jumbo cinnamon roll… or two.

"Why the double order?"

"30 hours. Long trip."

"They serve food on the planes, you know."

"Pbtht! Who can eat that crap?"

I couldn't argue with that. Besides, Dan knew I could polish off even a double order because he'd witnessed my eating exploits numerous times. Like our after-school end-of-the-season 8th-grade basketball party. Dan watched as I ate eight hot dogs with buns, two bags of potato chips, a jar of pickles, and a stack of cookies. He didn't see what I then had for dinner at home - two cheeseburgers, a plate of fries, a salad (have to eat something healthy), and a piece of apple pie for dessert, a la mode, of course.

In high school, Dan watched as I, with his help, helped clean out his parent's freezer. After Dan got a car, sometimes he'd drive home for lunch, sometimes with me along for the ride. With his parents at work, the house empty, he'd pop a couple of frozen pizzas into the oven.

I'd eat mine… and half of his.

Then he looked to see what else he could find in the freezer that needed eating. Even though his parents had a well-stocked freezer, they usually dined out, so there wasn't much turnover.

"Here's a box of Fudgsicles from last year's family reunion nobody ate," tossing them in my general direction.

"They're way past the expiration date."

"Na-nah. They're still good."

"OK."

After finishing the box, he stuck his head in the freezer, looking for more food his parents wouldn't miss. So, a few years later, it was no surprise that Dan made a career in the restaurant business because ensuring people had plenty to eat seemed important to him.

For as much as I'd eat for lunch at his parent's house and for breakfast, lunch, or dinner in his restaurant, it wasn't as much as I sometimes eat as a dinner guest in Dan and wife Marsha's home. More than a few times, I could barely drive myself home, essentially "food drunk."

If the police ever pulled me over, I would've passed a breathalyzer test with ease, but other field tests, like balancing on one foot, walking heel to toe along a straight line, or remaining conscious? I'm not so sure because, at Dan and Marsha's home, there's not only great food but also lots of it, and no such thing as leftovers. Any food they put on the dinner table is meant to be eaten - right then, right there. Why theirs is likely a Tupperware-free home. Knowing I can and do clean my plate, Dan piles any would-be leftovers onto mine.

"C'mon Johnny, finish'er up!"

And I always do.

103

IT'S JUST POOP

For eleven years, part of my job description was cleaning toilets. Eleven years. So when I retired at 44, a quarter of my life had been spent in restrooms, cleaning up after others, for money...

"Toilet whore!" Sue, again, likes to contribute...

For ten of those eleven years, the toilets were in a bar (and restaurant), and you know how unclean those are at closing time. I've seen things... and done things... all valid reasons why I never saw the need to "apologize" for retiring way early.

You never really know how far your arm can go down a toilet until it's your job to unplug it. So, in Al Ain, I could relate to a guy I knew named Guy, an Australian camel vet. Breeding racing camels for the royal family of Abu Dhabi, a major part of his job was to inseminate them artificially. The camels, not the royal family. The best way to do that was by hand.

"How was work today, Guy?"

"Up to me shoulders in camel jut, mate."

There were other bathrooms, those onboard the Chief Waupaca, the authentic sternwheel paddleboat I piloted for ten years. Tiny bathrooms, similar in size to those on a commercial airliner, they could get awful rank during daytime public tours, but since most days ended with three-hour private charters, ones which often featured alcohol… I've seen things… and done things… especially after wapatuli parties.

If you're unfamiliar with wapatuli, recipes vary, but it's a drink consisting of cut-up fresh fruit, fruit juice, and alcohol. A lot of alcohol because wapatuli, customarily made only for parties, is often mixed in 30-gallon plastic garbage cans, clean ones, of course.

My Uncle Mike says those wapatuli parties are called "Purple Jesus" if you use grape juice. He also says that when the alcohol is Japanese cooking sake, the hurls can be spectacular. It's purple, and for anyone who ever drank Japanese cooking sake and then hurled, a common comment afterward was, "Jesus, what's in that stuff?" Hence, Purple Jesus.

With the right recipe, drinkers don't taste the alcohol, so it goes down like Kool-Aid. And that's the problem because wapatuli can come up as easily as it goes down. Far too often, passengers got over-the-top intoxicated… and over-the-side sick… why I had to hose vomit off the sides of the Chief, as well as every other surface. With a wapatuli party, my night was not over after passengers stumbled off the boat because I didn't dare let the sticky mess dry overnight. Not only was spilled wapatuli - before and after it was drunk - challenging to clean once dried, it attracted flies like fresh manure only wishes it could.

Someone, someone had to clean it up and that someone was me. Besides, I knew there weren't many, if any, I worked with who would, you know, volunteer to help, including our bouncer, a guy named Thor. As you might expect, given he was a bouncer, named Thor, he was a big guy, but when it came to such things, he was as squeamish as a girly girl holding a wiggling worm.

Every summer for a few years, Thor hosted a charter on the Chief, a wapatuli party. One night, some young lady had already had too much to drink less than an hour into the cruise and hurled into a cardboard box filled with bags of Delicious-brand, made-in-Waupaca potato chips. The chips inside the sealed bags were fine, but no one was willing to clean the mess to get to them. So when the charter was over, the bags of chips were still in the box. So was her vomit. Wapatuli does make for some colorful puke.

That's when Thor approached, asking, somewhat sheepishly, "John, can you do me a favor? Please?"

"Sure, Thor. Whaddya need?" because I liked Thor.

So, after reminding me how he didn't have the stomach for such things and knowing I did, he asked if I would clean the mess, saving the case of otherwise edible potato chips.

"Sure, Thor, no problem," because I liked Thor.

After dumping the bags on the dock, I turned the hose on them, washing the regurgitated wapatuli into the lake. Even in the dark, the bluegills were right there, keeping their lake clean. Some no doubt got their first taste of wapatuli that night, feeling fine for the experience. And if they threw it up, "Jesus, what's in that stuff?"

As I washed the bags, Thor apologized profusely for asking such a favor.

"Not a problem, Thor. Really."

I put the cleaned bags into a different box and handed it to him.

"Thor, one thing though…"

"Sure, John. What?"

"Don't tell anyone what happened to these chips… until after they've eaten them."

"Will do!"

"Then tell me about it."

I had some comedy relief before the hard work began because I hosed the boat from stem to stern by the light of the dock spotlight. The Chief would still require further cleaning in the morning, but at least the before-bed bath removed the first and worst layer of slime. The boat's owner, Pat, eventually added a $100 cleaning fee for wapatuli parties, but I never saw a penny, except for the extra hours of pay I received cleaning up the mess.

Then there were the restrooms. If I never see, much less clean another chemical toilet… But it wasn't just the toilets that needed cleaning, as the onboard septic tank needed to be pumped. While it may not sound so, this was the most pleasant part of the clean-up… unless something went wrong.

If it did, it was almost always because someone put something into the toilet they had not drunk or eaten first. That something something I'd have to extract from the pump's impeller (your vocabulary word for the day) after disconnecting the hoses, ones filled with chemically treated sewage. I was always careful, but sometimes, some would spill into the lake. While a Department of Natural Resources warden wouldn't have liked that, the bluegills that lived under the dock loved it, "Jesus, what's in that stuff!" no kid with a 5-cent cup of oatmeal ever getting such an enthusiastic response.

Then there was the time the Chief's septic tank developed a leak, the bottom rusted "clean" through. The bluegills got no free meals since the tank leaked inside the boat's hull. So until we could get the steel tank repaired, every day for a week, I spent my mornings in the crawlspace under the lower deck, accessed by a hatch, cleaning chemically treated sewage with a bucket and a sponge. Fortunately, the compartmentalized construction of the hull kept the ooze relatively well contained.

It was one of the few times I ever appreciated the Chief's flat bottom because, with no real keel, the wind steered the boat more than I did, especially during storms. Out on a charter one night, I got caught in a squall. Heading back to the dock because of too-close-for-comfort lightning strikes, as I made my approach, a half a lake away, Pat, a partying passenger that night, entered the pilot house.

"So, John… what's your plan for docking?"

He was concerned because it was his boat, his customers, and the wind was howling. For docking, my wind gauge was the Old Style beer sign hanging off a pole at the end of the next dock over from the Chief's. That night, Old Style was horizontal. With the nasty crosswind, I matter-of-factly told Pat, "I'm just gonna aim about three docks to the right." It seemed like a most excellent plan. Turned out it was because Pat was impressed after I stuck the landing.

"Sure am glad you were driving tonight, John."

So was I, especially since Pat had been thoroughly enjoying the party. But not so much that he didn't remember my matter-of-factly "aim about three docks to the right" remark because years later, I learned he'd repeated the comment several times as an example of why he never worried when I was piloting his boat, insured for over a million dollars.

But then I've repeated his "character builder" comment several times over the years. That remark, made after the fourth of four public sightseeing tours, has stuck with me, and so too has the character-building episode that prompted it, which happened after the third tour that day.

I always disliked the third tour.   If it were a workday, the third tour would've been a Wednesday - hump day - I sometimes finding it hard to remember if I'd said parts of the tour spiel already, or was that the last tour?   And this particular third tour was the worst ever, although I wouldn't know it until it was over.   In addition to the usual walk-on passengers, onboard that day was a bus group out for a day trip of east-central Wisconsin tourist traps.

Sitting in the pilot house on the upper deck, I had no way of knowing what was happening in the cabin below unless it was something I could hear or feel.   So I had no reason to believe anything untoward had occurred as I greeted passengers stepping off the boat and onto the dock… until the tour manager of the bus group informed me one of her charges had "discharged" herself in the lower cabin.   So before allowing the next group to board, I closed the gate, politely telling them there would be a short delay.

"Don't worry.   You'll still get the full hour-and-a-half tour."

I don't know what I expected to find when I entered the carpeted cabin, but I'm pretty sure it wasn't a trail of "butterscotch pudding" stretching from stern to stem where the boat's restrooms were.

"She just had to be sitting in the back row."

We kept cleaning supplies onboard for such emergencies.   I did the best I could, but unable to remove anything used to clean the mess without passing by the customers waiting on the dock, I threw it all in the bathroom she "used" and locked the door.   Because what she'd done in the bathroom made what she'd done in the cabin look almost presentable to the public.

"What the hell?   She should be in an ambulance, not on a tour bus."

Pat didn't pay me that much, but I never complained or asked for a raise because it was a job I treasured. That day, though, I was tempted to ask, simply because I knew few others other than me could and would do the necessary.

And after the final tour of the day, after I cleaned the mess in the bathroom, there was Pat, in the ticket booth to greet me with a gargantuan grin on his face. Therese, "The Queen of the Ticket Booth," had cued him in on my between-tours cleanup in aisle one.

"John! Heard you had a character-builder today!"

And I did. While I'm sure others would've quit that day, such things never really bothered me.

It's just poop.

104

HOW COLD IS?

"Mister John, what you eat for breakfast?"

"Most mornings, I have a bowl of cereal and peanut butter toast."

"Sir, what peanut butter?"

Way back when, peanut butter was not the ubiquitous item in the United Arab Emirates that it was in the States. Nevertheless, the question, "What peanut butter?" caught me off guard because I couldn't imagine the young ladies in my class at UAE University not knowing what it was when I'd been smearing the stuff since I was old enough to wield a (peanut) butter knife.

"It's like butter, but thicker and brown because it's made with peanuts instead of milk."

"Ewwwww! Baby poop, sir."

Why, for a while, I put other favorites (cinnamon and honey) on my toast - cleaning poop one thing, but the idea of eating it quite another. Peanut butter was easy enough to explain, but given that it was rarer than a white man in Al Ain, it wasn't until I brought a jar to class that I was convinced my students knew what it was.

My students had questions, many of which had nothing to do with the curriculum. I also had questions, as my students and I were curious about each other's culture years before the Internet came along and provided... clarity. Many of their questions were inspired by what they saw watching American TV and movies, the 1996 film *Fargo*, for example...

"Sir, why they talk funny?"

That led to a short lesson on regional accents in the States, ending with my question, "Does everyone in the UAE speak Arabic the same?"

"No, sir."

"Not everyone in the States speaks English the same either."

Knowing my propensity to speak in voices other than my own, one student asked, "Sir, can you talk like the Fargo people?"

"Like diss, yah mean? Yah dare hay!"

Once the laughter subsided, more questions followed, "Sir, everyone have wood chipper?"

"No... fortunately."

In *Fargo*, what piqued the interest of my desert-dwelling students most was the winter weather.

"This like where you from, Mister John?"

"Yes, in winter. Not all year... it just seemed that way..."

"What, sir?"

"Nothing..."

"Sir, how you live in snow?"

"Same way you live in sand, you just do."

"How you live in cold?"

"Wear more clothes, heat instead of air condition buildings, and same as here, complain a lot, only that it's too cold instead of too hot."

Many of my Emirati students hadn't received the best primary and secondary school education, but they were generally curious. They always had questions and weren't afraid to ask, a difference I noticed living in Ecuador, where the locals mostly didn't ask. Given that some of our neighbors know little more than the valley where they live, they probably don't know enough to ask or enough to be curious.

The most challenging question regarding the weather was, "How cold is?" How could I explain cold, extreme cold, to my Emirati students when most had never experienced temperatures anywhere close to freezing? When it came to peanut butter, I could bring in a jar so my students could see, smell, feel, and even taste it. But cold? I couldn't bring bitter cold to show and tell in one of the hottest places on earth.

Mentally flipping through my inventory of stories, I found one involving cold, and a wedding, sure to get the attention of any young Emirati woman.

"You want to know how cold is? The day my stepbrother…"

"Mister John, what stepbrother?"

"A stepbrother is a brother by marriage, not by birth. He has a different set of parents."

An in-the-know student explained to the rest of the class, in Arabic, what I'd said, buttressing my explanation. The knowing nods that followed told me I could continue…

"The day my stepbrother got married, the temperature was minus 40 (-40F)."

"Minus 40! Sir!"

"With the wind chill, it was even colder."

"Wind chill?"

"When it's cold, wind makes the air feel even colder."

"Dirty trick, sir."

"Yes, that's why anyone with any sense got married in summer, not winter. But on January 9, 1977, in Eau

Claire, where I was born, the city set a record for Wisconsin's lowest ever temperature... the day my stepbrother got married."

"Silly man."

"Yes... yes, he was. You know what happens when it's minus 40?"

"What, sir?"

"When you exhale, you can see your breath freeze after it leaves your mouth. You can hear it, too. Your face freezes in seconds, making it difficult to speak."

"That why they talk funny in *Fargo*?"

"Yes... one reason anyway. When it's really cold, sometimes you can't start your car because it's frozen."

"Frozen, sir?"

"Yes, the fuel, oil, and water can freeze if it gets too cold. That's why, where I come from, many people plug in their cars to keep them warm."

"You plug in the car? Like hair dryer?"

"Yes, where it's cold, many cars have electric heaters to keep the engine from freezing when you park a car overnight."

"That not a problem here, sir."

"No, but there are other problems, different problems."

"What, Mister John?"

"Once, after I parked my car in the sun, a water bottle I'd left on the front seat fell against the door. By the end of the day, the bottle top had melted into the door."

"Hot here, sir."

"Why my car key burned my fingers after I took it out of the ignition."

"Very hot here, sir."

"Yes, why sometimes I can't hold the steering wheel... and my backside burns on the seat."

"Yes! Big problem, sir!" exclaimed one student as her hands smacked her ample hips.

"The morning of the wedding was so cold we could only start one car. All the rest were dead."

"Dead?"

"Wouldn't start. Turn the key… nothing. Frozen."

"No one plug them in, sir?"

"Just too cold, even with heaters. So we had to make many trips to get everyone to the church. It was a bumpy ride because the tires were frozen."

"Tires freeze too, sir?"

"Yes. When you park a car, the part of the tire on the road is flat. When it's that cold, the tires freeze, so when you drive, every time those flat spots roll around, it's like hitting a speed bump."

"I never know this, sir."

"Why would you? It never gets close to freezing here. That day, it was minus 40."

"How cold is?"

And we were right back where we started because despite their questions and my answers, a classroom of ladies who'd likely never seen anything colder than sweater weather still did not understand how cold minus 40 was. I was frustrated because I wanted them to know, I wanted them to understand the weather they'd seen in *Fargo*, weather that impressed them enough to ask their teacher. So how could they experience what they never had, maybe never would?

"Ladies, when you go home this weekend, go to the kitchen, your refrigerator, and open the freezer door. Stick your head inside. Stand on a chair if you need to. Close the door as far as you can. Keep your head in there as long as you can. While doing that, hold a tub of ice cream or something for as long as you can so your hands feel the cold."

"Homework, Mister John?"

"Yes, homework!"

The following week, I was curious to see if anyone had done their "homework." A few had. Others were tempted, I'm sure, but didn't, perhaps out of fear over what their family might think, especially their father...

"Maryam! What are you doing?"

"Mister John told me to put my head in the freezer."

"Mister John? Who is this Mister John? That sounds like a man!" (Some students didn't want their father to know a man, much less a Western man, was teaching them for fear that their father might remove them from the university.)

"Yes, my teacher at the university."

"He told you to put your head in the freezer?"

"Yes, so I could see how cold is."

I should mention that in the UAE, higher education at government-run colleges and universities was free to all Emiratis, so... no refunds...

I asked one student who'd done her homework, "How cold is?"

"I don't breathe. My hands cold, but they burn. Very strange, Mister John."

"So you didn't like the cold?"

"NO!"

"You know what the temperature was in your freezer? Around minus 18 (0F)... probably warmer since your head was in there and the door was open. How cold was it when my stepbrother got married?"

"Minus 40 (-40F), sir."

"So the day my stepbrother got married, it was 22 (40F) degrees colder than inside your freezer."

"Crazy. Better you live here, Mister John."

"Yes... yes, it is."

105

THE FIRST THING I KNEW

They're some of my favorite people and some of the best supporters of my writing and photography. They've also proven a valuable resource, teaching me more, for starters, about Black History, a state I knew almost nothing of - West Virginia, and raising turtles. They've provided me a window to life, past and present, in places ranging from rural Wisconsin to Australia and in homes shared with known knowns.

They're the social media friends I've never met. Even so, I know more about them than some people I have met, people I've known for years, even people I'm related to. Yes, thanks to social media, I know what they look like, what they used to look like. I know where they've lived, worked, and attended school. I know their political and religious views. I know what businesses and causes they support. What hangouts they frequent. Where they vacation. What they like to eat. I know their favorite books, movies, and TV shows, along with their favorite performers. I know their pets and their names. I even know some of their family and friends.

I hope governments and corporations don't catch on to this because those are only the highlights.

For everything I know about those I know thanks to social media but have never met, there's one thing I don't know - what they sound like. My, oh my, how communication has changed, because I remember when the only thing I knew about someone I'd never met, never even seen, was what they sounded like, one of those earliest someones, Elton John. When I was transitioning to teenager, he was at the pinnacle of his career, the biggest rock star on the planet. He's been around so long that it's easy to forget how big Elton was back in the 70's.

After its May 19, 1975 release, his album *Captain Fantastic and the Brown Dirt Cowboy* debuted on the U.S. Billboard Chart at #1, staying there for seven weeks. His next album, *Rock of the Westies* (a play on "West of the Rockies" and like *Captain Fantastic*, recorded at the Caribou Ranch in Colorado) also debuted at #1 after its October 24 release. In the days before social media, no album had ever debuted at #1, and Elton had two in a row turn the trick. On October 25 and 26, he packed Dodger Stadium in Los Angeles with 55,000 fans - they there to see him and only him, at the time, the largest concerts ever for a single artist.

The year before, when I was 12 years old, I acquired my first album, *Elton John's Greatest Hits*, a Christmas present picked out by me and paid for by Ma. Released in November of 1974, the cover and jacket photos were the first I'd seen of Elton John. That's right, despite his success, I had no idea what he looked like. Imagine that. Given his over-the-top getups and glasses, I still didn't know what he looked like.

Even before my time, not knowing was a thing. Just ask the promoter who booked Buddy Holly & The Crickets to play at Harlem's Appollo Theater. He assumed they were black, which happened on occasion since most acts were heard before they were seen. FYI, despite the "error," the audience loved the show.

What I knew was what Elton sounded like, and then only when singing. Later, I was surprised to hear him speak on TV in an English accent because he didn't sing with one. A year or so later, I learned his real name was Reginald Dwight. I shrugged, understanding why, as a rock star in the making, he might want to change his name. A decade or so later, I learned he was gay. Again, I shrugged, his music sounding the same that day as it always had.

While I didn't know much about Elton John, not nearly what I know about my social media friends, even those I've never met, at least I would've had some conversation starters had we met. Otherwise, our encounter would've been awkward because as little as I knew about the "Rocket Man," he would've known nothing about me, why I've always been ill-at-ease meeting new people because I know nothing about them.

When I get to know them, though, I usually get to know the basics, the answers to all the usual questions - Where are you from? What do you do? Are you married? While it could take years, maybe most of a lifetime, to get to know some people well, there are still some things, personal things, you'll likely never know.

There are, however, exceptions, like the woman I first saw while waiting for an elevator in Sharjah's Canal Building. No, not Sue - because I met her in the same building while waiting for an elevator - but another woman whose name I would never know. The wait would've been a typically uneasy one - two strangers close, with nothing to talk about - but our limited time together was more awkward than usual, for me anyway, the ride down more so, owing to the first thing I knew about her, learned in the middle of the night before.

There were so many things I wanted to say, was tempted to say, dying to say, but didn't, before she exited at the ground floor lobby, before I continued to the basement parking garage. Given her lack of shame, our brief elevator encounter wasn't any more awkward than usual for her, unless she had no shame, because the first thing I knew about my neighbor's girlfriend was what she sounded like in his bed, engaged in sexual intercourse.

Yup, the night before, I knew one and only one thing about her, rarely the first thing anyone knows about another person. Some spouses don't even know what their partner sounds like in the throes of passion, yet I knew what this woman sounded like... and nothing else... until I saw her in the hallway the following morning, waiting for the elevator. Where I wondered.... Would she recognize herself if I started doing an impersonation of her from the night before? And if she did, what would she do?

Despite what I'd heard the night before, I never said a word, remembering where I was, not just in a hallway, waiting for an elevator, but in a conservative Muslim country. That was the only time I ever saw her, although I heard her a few more times. Then, the other side of the shared bedroom wall went quiet for a while, so I assumed she and my neighbor had broken up. I felt bad for him because it sounded like she was really into him... and he... into her.

I did not know whether he lost any sleep over the breakup with his ex-girlfriend, but I know I enjoyed a month of uninterrupted sleep... until he got a new girlfriend... or so I heard.

106

DEAD DUCK

"Why do you want to hurt my ducks? What did they ever do to you?"

They were just ducks. I was just a little kid. They were teenagers, throwing rocks at the ducks. I wanted them to stop but was too scared to say anything. Looking around for help, I saw a woman about Ma's age reading a book on a nearby park bench, so I ran to her for help.

"Please! Make those boys stop throwing rocks at the ducks! Please!"

She raised her head above the top of her book just enough to see the goings-on in the creek before her.

"I didn't know they were throwing rocks at the ducks," her nose then returned to the pages of her book.

"Why don't you make them stop?"

With barely a turn of her head, she said, "They're just ducks," then resumed reading.

"What is wrong with you?"

"They're just… ducks."

In Bloomer, Wisconsin, a town of 2000 in northwest Wisconsin, the dam - and the creek below - was one of my favorite places, a magnet when I'd visit my Grandpa and Grandma Wall. Located just three blocks from their home on Oak Street, I couldn't wait to get to the dam when I visited. All that water held behind a concrete wall so tranquil, and what overflowed the spillway, the supply seemingly never-ending, kept the creek below flowing, even if ever so slowly.

While the dam didn't move, and the creek below only enough the ducks needed but an occasional paddle to hold their positions, the setting changed with Wisconsin's distinctive seasons. Fitting it was autumn, with most everything except for the evergreens dead or dying when those teenagers were throwing rocks at the ducks.

Until it was just one duck separated from the flock.

Knowing the duck was vulnerable only seemed to "inspire" those teenagers more, for with "blood in the water," the intensity of their rock-throwing increased. I watched in utter anguish. There were so many of them, and only one of me, along with one apathetic bookworm. Even so, to this day, I wish I'd found the courage to say something, to scream something, anything. Maybe it would've been enough for evil not to triumph that day... or maybe it would've caused those monsters to turn their attention to the little kid... the one with a breaking heart.

After those teenagers so severely wounded the duck that their "joy" in tormenting it ceased, they wandered off, no doubt to make more trouble. With them out of sight, I rushed to the riverbank, the wounded duck floundering, barely, on the far side of the creek and out of my reach. Knowing every second could mean the difference between life and death, my anguish spiked, it taking forever for the slow-flowing creek to finally catch and then carry the duck downstream.

Once it did, I followed, under bridges and around bends, the wounded duck always, excruciatingly, just out of reach. Whatever little life it had at the beginning of our journey appeared to have left it. Finally, finally, just outside of town, near the high school, the creek then just a few feet wide, I was able to reach the duck and pull it from the water, its neck… broken… its life… lost.

Holding the duck by its broken neck to keep its feet from dragging on the ground, I carried it through Bloomer to my grandparent's house on the other side of downtown. Tears streaming down my face, I was heartbroken for the duck… and to learn it wasn't the monsters under my bed I needed to worry about.

"How could they be so mean?"

They weren't the only ones because, during the walk to my grandparents, I passed a home where one of a half-dozen or so "people" on the front porch asked, "What's wrong, little boy?"

"The duck is dead," I said.

Their laughter told me they didn't care. It was just a duck. A dead duck. Even after I arrived at my grandparent's house, even with it full of family, my walking in the front door holding the dead duck seemed to be the problem, not why it was dead, no one even asking. Big people took the duck from me and buried it in my grandparent's garden. They then returned to their Thanksgiving Day celebrations. I was left standing there… empty-handed.

It was just a duck. A dead duck. Why, the next day, when I returned to the scene of the crime, there was one less duck in the creek below the dam. Not that anyone would notice. Not that I would've noticed if not for what I'd seen and experienced the day before. A boy so young shouldn't have to learn he couldn't fix dead, that he couldn't fix a broken neck… or broken people.

Maybe it was better to learn early on of the evil within some, often magnified in groups. I was too young then to know of Nazis, the slave trade, genocide, gulags, and other human atrocities. After I learned, I wasn't surprised, as school bullies were a near-constant reminder that some people would be cruel simply because they could be - that perhaps the only source of joy in their otherwise miserable ~~lives~~ existence.

107

NO CHRISTMAS TREE?

If a dilapidated bus rumbled through your small town in central Wisconsin on a sunny summer day with a bunch of teenagers hanging out the windows screaming at the top of their lungs, you'd probably shrug it off, "Kids these days."

Unless that small town was Plainfield, Wisconsin, former home to one of America's most notorious psycho killers, Ed Gein.

The inspiration for the Norman Bates character portrayed by Anthony Hopkins in the Alfred Hitchcock movie classic *Psycho*, Ed Gein confessed to killing only two women, one in 1954 and another in 1957. Instead, it was his highly disturbing collection of grave-robbed "memorabilia" that made him infamous.

Initially, he was found mentally incompetent to stand trial. "Ya think?" But later, Ed was tried for the 1957 murder and received a life sentence. And it was, as he died in 1984 while incarcerated at the Mendota Mental Health Institute in Madison, Wisconsin.

Despite Plainfield's proximity to Waupaca, about 25 or so miles to the southwest, it's not really on the way to anywhere, so I've only been there a couple of times - once for a basketball game and the other, on that bus full of screaming teenagers.   Teenagers with inquiring minds… and questions for the locals…

"WHERE'S ED?"

"ARE YOU ED?"

"IS THAT ED'S HOUSE?"

"WAS ED YOUR BABYSITTER?"

"ARE YOU ED'S LOVE CHILD?"

Me?   I just sat there, minding my own business. Or maybe that was the weirdo seated next to me…

Screaming questions or not, all of us on the bus were employees of Kirk's Christmas Trees, located about halfway between Wild Rose and Wautoma, 20-some miles south of Waupaca. The Wautoma Plantation was once the largest of Kirk's operations, covering more than ten thousand acres and planted with millions of trees. Trees that needed trimming every summer after their spring growth spurt.

Working for Kirk's wasn't my first choice. It wasn't any choice for the many Mexican migrant workers in the area, as all preferred to work on their hands and knees, picking beans. Kirk's was the worst job I've ever had, and considering part of my job description for the next ten summers was cleaning toilets and pumping sewage, that's saying something.

But as I was moving to Florida at the end of July, there weren't many half-summer jobs available, so I signed on - beggars can't be choosers and all that. The six weeks of seasonal work would allow me to earn some money before beginning my freshman year at the University of Florida - out-of-state tuition and all that.

Kirk's was trying to make money, too, and apparently didn't mind bending the rules to boost their profit margin. Most of the buses they used to transport their workers had a maximum capacity of 54. Kirk's seemed to regard that as a suggestion because they stuffed their buses as full as possible to reduce transportation costs.

Occasionally, the local police would pull over a bus and hand the driver a ticket for exceeding the "Max Cap." After a short delay, the bus would continue on its way. The police never demanded Kirk's bring out another bus and split the load. Backroom agreement?

For Kirk's, a citation was probably just another business expense, cheaper than buying more buses and paying more drivers. And if you ever drove through nearby Wild Rose one mile per hour above the posted speed limit, 25mph, you're probably aware of how the local police force supplemented their budget.

Most of Kirk's buses were 1950s models that had long been deemed unfit to haul school children, but for a rag-tag bunch of teenage Christmas tree trimmers? Perfect! Driven to remote fields, we'd pile off the bus, happy for fresh air and elbow room.

Once recombobulated, we'd size up the field before us. Some only took a few hours to trim before we were back on the bus and off to another field. Good, because that bus ride was on the clock. But some fields, the ones where we couldn't see the ends of the rows, took days, not hours, to trim.

"Well... we know where we're gonna be this week."

We'd all pick a row, spacing ourselves a row apart. Alternating rows not only for safety reasons - teenagers with machetes - but also so we wouldn't waste time walking back when we reached the end of a row. Instead, we had a return row to trim. "Right turn, Clyde."

Our tedious trimming aimed to make the trees Christmas-worthy by shaving the new growth off the sides, creating that classic conical shape. Stunting the outward growth also encouraged the trees to fill in so they'd be bushy. The tricky part was the top. While all lateral buds were to be trimmed, the terminal bud, the top of the trunk, was not to be cut, or it would branch out, resulting in a tree with multiple tops. Since most families only had one star to top their Christmas tree, Kirk's wanted Christmas trees with only one top.

Precise aim with a machete was required to trim the branches surrounding the top without slicing it off. Since many lacked that, in the hand not holding the machete, trimmers held a wooden-handled metal stem with a hook on the end to pull the terminal bud out of the machete's path. Tops still got topped. It was an easy way to end your day, even your "career" at Kirk's. After topping one too many trees, a trimmer could spend the rest of the day on the bus, unpaid. Or worse, they'd be fired. Especially if the trees were the larger, more valuable ones, or the field supervisor was suffering from a nasty hangover.

Most of Kirk's trees were seven years old or less, as they planted trees in an eight-year cycle. After harvesting a field, they left it dormant for a year, then planted seedlings, the resulting trees trimmed each year for seven years - the time it takes to get a floor-to-ceiling Christmas tree - before they'd repeat the cycle.

But in some fields, there were sections with larger trees, ones Kirk's allowed to grow for more than seven years, selling those trees to churches, banks, and other such establishments with greater floor-to-ceiling heights. Of course, those trees were worth much more than the typical household Christmas tree.

Regarded as one of the better trimmers, I was requested to trim such trees a few times. And when it came time to trim those high-end trees, field supervisors would awaken from their slumber to ensure the job was done right, short of doing it themselves. Despite knowing I was about to trim a tree that would sell for hundreds of dollars, often the only instruction I got from those supervisors was… "Don't fuck it up!"

Adding to the degree of difficulty, the tops of those trees couldn't be trimmed while standing on the ground. So I had to climb them, careful not to break any branches along the way. Once close enough to the top, I'd grab the trunk with my left hand and lean back as far as possible to trim the top with the machete in my right. With my two hands already occupied, the hook could not be used, so I had to be even more careful with my aim, even though I was hanging precariously off the side of a bendy tree.

The job had other hazards, too, as sunburn and dehydration were common. Once in a while, someone would step on an anthill in the sandy soil, the severity of the situation measured in "curse words per minute." And some trimmers just never got their head wrapped around the fact that if any part of their body crossed their machete's path, they'd slice themselves.

I never did, but one day, I halved a hornet's nest hidden in a tree I was trimming. I didn't notice it until the hornets pointed it out to me, furious I'd just turned their basketball-sized single-family home into a duplex. While my clothing provided some protection from their stinging protests, I knew it wouldn't be enough.

Over the buzz of the angry and growing mob, I heard the sound of spraying water, "Irrigation!" the bean field next to ours being watered. So, with hornets hot on my trail, I raced down my row, hurdled the barbed wire fence separating the fields, and positioned myself under the shower of water until the hornets gave up their quest for revenge.

When I returned to my row, a passing field supervisor noticed I was soaking wet with not a cloud in the sky. "What's up with... this?" So I explained what had happened, pointing to the irrigation still in progress. He grunted, "Work through your next water break." Hard to argue with that logic.

Kirk's sent busses to surrounding communities to collect workers. I'm not sure they would've had many if they hadn't gone out of their way to get them. For me, it was a half-hour ride to Kirk's headquarters, where I was then redirected to another bus that would take me and other trimmers out to the fields. By the time I was on the clock, I'd already put in an hour on two of Kirk's dilapidated buses.

We worked from eight until noon with a legally mandated 15-minute water break at ten. One of the higher-ups, who'd made a career of bossing teenagers during the summer, would come by in a pickup truck with water coolers and a supply of paper cups. If we were lucky, another flunky would sharpen our machetes during the break.

The machete I've used for all my years in Ecuador cost only four dollars, plus an additional twenty-five cents for a guy to grind an edge on the new blade, I not yet having a grinder of my own. Despite the low, low price, it's a far better machete than those Kirk's supplied their workers. Resembling a large cake-frosting knife, Kirk's machetes only held an edge for a few trees, and then it was back to whacking away with a fairly dull blade until the next sharpening.

Given a half-hour for lunch, we had to brown bag it as dining options in the remote fields were non-existent. There was another water break at two-thirty. Quitting time was four-thirty. During that last half hour, time moved more slowly than it does sitting in a dentist's chair on the receiving end of a root canal. I'd trim and trim and trim... "4:08? You gotta be kidding

me!"   So I'd trim and trim and trim some more…
"OK, surely now it must be quitting time…   4:14.
Sonofabitch!"

The pay was minimum wage, $3.35 an hour. If a
field supervisor decided I had a good day trimming
trees, for that day, he could bump me up to $3.55, or
even $3.75 an hour… and into a higher tax bracket. At
quitting time, it was a half-hour bus ride back to Kirk's
and then another half-hour bus ride back to fabulous
downtown King. A half-mile or so walk from there,
and I'd be home by six, on a good day.

My first day working at Kirk's was not one such
day because the bus broke down on the ride back to
King, about halfway between Wild Rose and Rural.
Given the metal-on-metal grinding and banging that
preceded the wheels on the bus no longer going round
and round, I figured we'd gone as far as we were going
to go, our driver confirming as much after taking a look
under the hood.

"You guys might as well start walking. This bus
ain't goin' nowhere." So we started walking. In the days
before cell phones, there wasn't much else we could do.
Eight miles later, I finally made it home. Del's first
question was, "So, how was your first day at Kirk's?"
Immediately followed by Ma's, "Why are you so late?"
Before I had a chance to answer either came question
number three,

"What's wrong with your hand?"

"It sucked! The bus broke down between Wild
Rose and Rural, so I had to walk. And after holding a
machete all day, I can't straighten my fingers."

With that, I sat down to a cold dinner, fumbling
with silverware not shaped like a machete handle. I
then watched TV for a bit before heading to bed earlier
than usual, as I'd be hopping on the Kirk bus in

fabulous downtown King at seven in the morning… maybe. And it usually took until the next morning before I could straighten my fingers, just in time to return to work.

The following summer was the first of my ten years working as captain of the sternwheeler Chief Waupaca, a job I dearly loved. But working at Clear Water Harbor wasn't always peachy-keen - cleaning up gallons of sewage in the bilge from a leaky septic tank, dumpster-diving for a newlywed who accidentally threw away the stand for her catered wedding cake, picking up cigarette butts of smokers who viewed the world as their ashtray, cleaning diarrhea off the Chief's carpeted cabin floor… There were other such character builders, but you get the idea.

Perhaps my least favorite experience working at Clear Water Harbor was the two weeks I spent slogging in knee-deep muck to create a water volleyball court in Taylor Lake - if you enjoy playing there, you're effin' welcome. But despite the back-breaking work, despite the smell that could knock a buzzard off a manure wagon, despite the biting bugs, despite the smart-assed remarks hurled my way from customers overly enjoying themselves on the back bar, at my expense, for the first time I told myself something I would forever repeat when faced with an onerous task, "It beats working at Kirk's."

That sentiment is a major reason why there's never been a Christmas tree in my house.

108

DEREK

Sue and I had never met Derek, but we had heard about him. Derek was a young man who moved into a house across the street from Sue's father, Art, in Calgary's Haysboro neighborhood, developed in the late 1950s. A building contractor, Art was responsible for the construction of many of the basements in the neighborhood, including his own, so Haysboro was not only Art's home since 1958, but it was also a major part of his legacy.

As a contractor, Art was a hands-on kind of guy, always busy doing something. Seldom did he sit still as idle hands made for an unhappy Art. And perhaps owing to his many years managing construction crews, he was happy only if those around him were busy too. But as Art grew older and his body began to break down, he simply couldn't do all the things he used to do, and with exacting standards, Art was seldom satisfied with those he hired to do what he no longer could.

During calls with her father, "lazy" and "incompetent" were two words Sue often heard as Art referred to his hired help… until Derek came along. Art described him as a beanpole, perhaps two meters

(6'8") tall, a skinny kid with a big smile and a friendly disposition. Much to Art's (and Sue's) delight, Derek did many of those chores around the house - like cleaning the roof gutters - he no longer could. And Derek completed those tasks to Art's satisfaction, which was no small feat.

While Art always found a way to reimburse him for his efforts, Derek's motivation was not monetary but to help a neighbor and a friend in need. From Sue's conversations with her father, it became increasingly clear that Derek had grown quite fond of the grumpy old man across the street.

Derek was the kind of neighbor everyone wished they had, as my friend Bill commented after reading an early draft of this story, "Everyone needs a Derek." He was undoubtedly the kind of neighbor Sue and her brother Scott wanted for their aging father, widowed when his wife, their mother, Patricia, unexpectedly passed away in 2003. But more importantly, they knew their father had a friend who would look in on him, even when his gutters didn't need cleaning.

While Art had plenty of friends up and down the block and across the alley out back, he spoke of Derek in a way he spoke of no other. Sharing an unlikely but special friendship they both treasured, they kept in touch even after Derek moved away.

In December 2013, Sue met Derek for the first time in her father's room at Calgary's Rockyview General Hospital. From those conversations with her father, Sue felt she already knew Derek and knew him well, so it was no surprise he'd made his way to the hospital to visit his failing friend. That's the kind of person he was, just as her father described.

Art was right about Derek's height, as he was a tall one and a bit on the thin side, perhaps a manifestation of Derek's health issues. Sue wasn't exactly sure what those issues were, but she was sure of one thing - Derek did indeed have a big heart.

Later that month, the day after Christmas, Art passed away. Four days after that, while Sue and Scott were rearranging the furniture in their father's house in preparation for the reception that would take place after the funeral the following day, they happened upon a card Derek sent to their father. Art kept the card right next to his computer, an "antique" iMac G4 that somehow still worked despite its advanced age.

The card included a handwritten note from Derek:

July 12, 2011
Dear Art,

You're probably sitting in your recliner right now, out of the hot sun, watching over the neighborhood. Hope your garden is full of potatoes and tomatoes, carrots and beets. I am in Northern B.C. right now and have crossed a lot of distance hiking through the Alpine in the Yukon. My group is 13 people strong, we have struggled through dense valleys filled with dwarf willow, climbed mountains in the rain, and crossed roaring wide rivers fed by glacial run-off. Already feeling the effects of change, this outdoor lifestyle is changing me for the better, giving me a deeper respect for the outdoors and a tolerance for adversity and uncertainty. We are traversing glaciers on rope teams and have yet to do whitewater canoeing, which sounds thrilling. Hope you have found another neighborhood kid to help mow your grass. I'll clean out your gutters when I get home in August.

Cheers, Derek.

So touched by the sincerity of Derek's friendship toward their father, Sue and Scott wanted to share his note at their father's funeral service, a service Derek would, of course, attend. The fact that Art not only kept the card but also kept it close showed how much Derek's friendship meant to him. Scott called Derek and explained how he and Sue had found his card and asked if they could read his note at the service the next day. Derek happily agreed.

But the next day, as the service was about to begin, Derek was nowhere to be found. Sue, Scott, and even the funeral director, having heard of Derek and his note, were becoming concerned. They waited as long as they could, but the service had to go on, including the reading of Derek's note. After the service concluded, departing mourners found the police waiting outside, hoping Derek would be in attendance. Seems he was missing, and the police also had an interest in what had become of him.

It wasn't until three days later that Sue and Scott learned why Derek had missed their father's funeral service. Derek had a big heart, but on December 31, the day of Art's funeral, that heart stopped beating. Derek was just 27 years old. Sadly, his health issues finally caught up with him on the very day his friend was laid to rest.

While the American media too often has a year-end fascination with celebrities who've passed away in the preceding year, I prefer to remember an ordinary person, an extraordinary ordinary person... Derek. His note to Art reflected the kind and caring person he was, one who made life for an older man whose children lived at a distance that much easier, that much better. Sue and Scott will always be grateful for Derek's presence in their father's life, and knowing how much Art would've missed him, they can only imagine how much Derek's family and friends must miss him.

THE END... OF THIS BOOK

THANK YOU!

Next in the series, **MISFIT 4**, has 36 more stories.

ENJOY!

MISTERJOHN.ME

yakpublishing.com

Milton Keynes UK
Ingram Content Group UK Ltd.
UKHW030853270924
448944UK00001B/17